Latter House Glory

Transformational Power for the Nations

Larry R. Taylor

Print Edition

Copyright © 2013 Larry Reagan Taylor

All rights reserved.
No part of this book may be reproduced in any form or by any electronic or mechanical means including information storage and retrieval systems, without permission in writing from the author. The only exception is by a reviewer, who may quote short excerpts in a review.

Unless otherwise noted, scripture taken from the New King James Version®. Copyright © 1982 by Thomas Nelson, Inc. Used by permission. All rights reserved.

ISBN-13: 978-1482331592
ISBN-10: 1482331594

Preface

Living in the Preamble

There are two clear biblical examples of living in the reality of what was coming next on God's calendar. King David raised a tabernacle in which worship was free and access to the Ark was open to all. Prior to the new covenant being established by Jesus, David lived and operated in a New Covenant reality. The other example is the disciples of Jesus who were sent out two by two and were given authority to operate in demonstrations of Kingdom power. Jesus imparted an anointing to them before the outpouring of the Holy Spirit on the day of Pentecost. They were operating in a coming dimension.

The Church of Jesus Christ is now called to operate in the same kind of "future living." Haggai says, "The glory of the latter house shall exceed the glory of the former house." There is a coming full and complete revelation of the glory of the Lord on the earth when the King of Glory returns to establish His reign physically on this earth. The "new heaven and earth" are not just going to be new as in starting over with a fresh replication of what now exists. The "new heaven and earth" will be new in kind, just as our bodies shall be "new" in the resurrection; not simply new in the chronological sense, but new in type. We will receive spiritual bodies designed for eternity and ultimate glory.

There is a group of people on the earth today who are commissioned to be a foretaste of that reality, a living tangible expression of the greatest glory that is to come. That group is called The Church. Not the institution of men, but the dynamic organic people of God indwelt and empowered by the Holy Spirit, the manifest presence of God. To live in that reality we must employ our access in the manner laid out in scripture, through the revelatory, transformational work of the Holy Spirit. Describing his own initial experience, Paul says that the gospel that He preached didn't come from man, but it came by the revelation of Jesus Christ (Gal. 1:11-12). Paul tells us that when the Holy Spirit turns on the revelatory light we see the reality of His glory now. The full revelation of the glory of the Father is seen in the face of Jesus Christ. In a preamble to the ultimate revelation for all of creation we are transformed into the image we behold (2 Corinthians 3:17-4:18).

It is in the times of intimacy with Jesus that we hear His voice, feel His touch and yes, see His face. As we draw close, we are changed by what we feel, hear and see. It is not emotionalism or allegory. We literally see, but we see in another realm; the glory realm. In the glory encounter we are not just changed into a better form of ourselves, we are transformed into "a new creature in Christ Jesus." It is beyond the capabilities of human flesh to traffic in that realm, so we are made into a new creation. Our new reality becomes, "it is no longer I that live, but Christ that lives within me..." As we "live and move and breathe and have our being in Him" we are living in the coming reality now.

To say something is spiritual does not mean that it is not literal. This is a mistaken understanding of "spiritual." C.S. Lewis described the heavenly reality as being more real than this earth. He spoke of grass in heaven as being hard as compared to earth grass because it was more, not less real. There is no contradiction in saying that something is spiritual and literal at the same time. Spiritual is literal, just in a different realm than we are used to operating. The main point here is this, as believers in Jesus Christ we have been given access and authority in a realm that the rest of humanity has not yet experienced. We are tasked with the amazing opportunity to live in ever increasing dimensions of glory as a manifested reality of that which is to ultimately come to the earth.

The Church is not on a down hill slide to oblivion, it is on the fast track of ever increasing glory culminating in the ultimate revelation of His glory on the earth in a spiritual and literal new day.

Changed Lives 9

Glory Encounters 11

   "...then God showed up." F. Gump ..13

   SHOW ME YOUR GLORY.................21

   GLORY IS THE GOAL......................36

   THE COVENANT OF GOODNESS...38

   THE REVIVAL CONNECTION..........41

   GOLD...43

   MEANWHILE, BACK AT THE RANCH   55

He Is Building A House 67

   IT ISN'T FINISHED..........................75

   IT'S GOING TO LOOK LIKE HIM ...80

   IT'S THE ANOINTING THAT MAKES THE DIFFERENCE....................................82

   INTENSITY 86

   "WE ARE YOUR TEMPLE..."...........88

Fellowship of the Mystery 93

   THE MYSTERY EXPOSED................95

    THE LATTER HOUSE GLORY 102

    HE IS BUILDING HIS CHURCH......107

    OUT OF THE SHADOWS 109

    UNSHAKEN 111

    THE MOVE IS ON 112

The Gospel of Glory 115

    THE GOODNESS OF GOD 117

    THE END GAME 120

    SILENCING THE CRITICS 123

Signs, Wonders and Miracles .127

    REALITY CHECK 134

    HIS GLORY..135

    DEAD FROG THEOLOGY.................139

    THE WORK OF AN EVANGELIST ...141

    GO MODE 144

    AT LAST 147

    WHEN THE GLORY COMES............149

    THE WOW FACTOR 152

    PREEMINENCE 154

Activating The Power 158

THE SPIRIT AND THE WORD *162*

TRANSFORMED BY HIS GLORY *167*

GREATER WORKS *170*

THREE THINGS *172*

TERRA FIRMA *174*

HE CALLS YOU SON *177*

FULLY PREACHED *178*

GLOBAL WEIRDING AND WOLVES   *181*

Portals of Glory 185

AN ISLAND EXPERIENCE *187*

WHAT ARE YOU EXPECTING? *189*

Introduction

Changed Lives

Is it biblical to follow signs and wonders? Are the stories of gold teeth, gold dust, feathers, oil and other unusual manifestations reported by hundreds of thousands of Christians all over the world true signs and wonders leading people to Jesus or false ones leading to deception? Is there a prophetic meaning for The Church and for you personally?

The bottom line is this; changed lives. Are lives being changed? One encounter with the glory of God will change your life forever. A lifestyle of glory encounters will transform your mind and conform you to the image of Christ. The purpose of this book is to lead you to your own personal glory encounters and give you greater understanding from a biblical perspective on how this fits in to God's ultimate plan for The Church. As you read these pages my prayer for you is found in Ephesians 1:17-22:

> "that the God of our Lord Jesus Christ, the Father of glory, may give to you the spirit of wisdom and revelation in the knowledge of Him, the eyes of your understanding being

enlightened; that you may know what is the hope of His calling, what are the riches of the glory of His inheritance in the saints, and what is the exceeding greatness of His power toward us who believe, according to the working of His mighty power which He worked in Christ when He raised Him from the dead and seated Him at His right hand in the heavenly places, far above all principality and power and might and dominion, and every name that is named, not only in this age but also in that which is to come. And He put all things under His feet, and gave Him to be head over all things to the church"

Chapter 1
Glory Encounters

In 1994 I experienced one of the most unusual weeks of my life. My wife Carol, our two daughters Leah and Anna, and I were staying in what we affectionately called "the compound." It was actually a farm in East Texas that was the home of a group that had responded to the leading of the Holy Spirit in the 1970s to establish a community of believers. Many of the group lived on the farm in the middle of the pine forest in the middle of nowhere. The meetinghouse and guesthouse were at the center of the farm. We were there to conduct revival meetings for the group, but as the week progressed I realized that I was the one getting the download this time.

I had been prompted by the Holy Spirit to pray and ask the Lord to teach me more about His glory that week. Although I had been a pastor for over 13 years and had a degree in religion from an accredited university, I had very little, if any, practical knowledge concerning the glory of the Lord. To be honest, the concept was pretty much meaningless to me. If I thought about it at all, I just consigned it to an eventual state in heaven or defined it according to what I had heard my college professors say based on the Hebrew; "**kabod**- weightiness; heaviness; all that God is." That definition seemed to me to be fairly generic and irrelevant to everyday life.

I guess what I was expecting was a theological understanding so that I could preach intelligently on the subject. What I got was far different. By the end of the week at "the compound" I realized God had sent me to His school of reality. Rather than simply giving me high sounding words, He gave me a week of hair-raising, nail biting, oh-my-gosh-what-was-that kind of experiences that I have since come to refer to as "glory encounters."

The lessons began with a focus on the Book of Ezekiel. God spoke to me to begin reading the whole book. As I began the project I first read the introduction in my study Bible, which said that among the Jews, Ezekiel is known as the prophet of God's glory. OK, that answered the question, "Why Ezekiel?" but much more was to come. In Ezekiel there are over 24 references to "glory." As I began to read the book, I realized that much of it was beyond my comprehension. To a child of the 60's it sounded like the account of a really wild drug trip or multiple encounters with alien extraterrestrials.

Little did I realize that I was about to see some of the events from the Book of Ezekiel duplicated in the real world where I was firmly planted in religious ignorance. What began to unfold in my life that week was the realization that God's glory is tangible and that every encounter with His glory is a life-altering, revelatory, transformational event.

"...THEN GOD SHOWED UP." F. GUMP

The night was hot and still. The roar of multiple electric fans was only a polite gesture of resistance against the matching 95% humidity and 95 degree temperature of deep East Texas. Accompanying the packed crowd of sweaty worshipers was the wall-to-wall volume of the fan motor choir joined by fiddles, accordions, trumpets, saxophone, guitars, piano, drums, tambourines and the thump/thump rhythm of a Fender bass set on ten and a half. Seated on the front row next to me, Carol had one simple prayer, "Lord, get me out of here."

As soon as the silent words were prayer-breathed through her lips, it happened. The way she describes it, suddenly she was someplace else. I was standing next to her so we know her physical body didn't leave the place, but she says it felt as if she literally left the room. I'll let her tell you the rest in her own words:

> Carol: "I was hot and tired, but did not want to embarrass Larry by walking outside to cool off, so I closed my eyes and raised my hands to at least give the appearance of worship. All of a sudden I felt like I was being lifted up and the sound of the music around me faded. I had seen visions during worship before,

but this was a new level for me. All I can say is that I felt like I was picked up and moved to a place very far away.

"I was standing at the edge of a large ballroom, dressed in a beautiful, white ruffled ball gown. The ballroom had a high, vaulted ceiling and was so large that I could not see the other side. The room was brightly lit, but I could not see any chandeliers or other sources of the bright light that filled the room. I could hear waltz music, but could not see an orchestra.

"As I stood there watching couples waltz to the beautiful music, I heard a voice say, 'Dance with me.' I turned around. There stood Jesus dressed in what I can only describe as a military officer's dress uniform. He took my hand and led me onto the dance floor. When we began to dance, I started laughing. I always loved watching people waltz, but never learned how myself.

"As we danced, Jesus said, 'Isn't my bride beautiful.' I looked up and saw the back of an elegant, white wedding dress with a long, white lace train. Jesus was suddenly standing by the bride and turned her toward me. As I looked, I saw that the dress was empty. Jesus was smiling and said, 'Soon I will come to get my bride.'

"Then I heard a loud, incredible sound. It sounded like singing with no discernible words. I know this sounds strange, but it was almost like I could taste the sweet sound. It got louder and louder until the sound shook my body, and I fell to my knees."

As I fell to my knees in the vision, I felt myself physically falling downward. I could hear the thump, thump sound of the bass and just as quickly as I left, I was back in the meetinghouse in East Texas. I was so 'drunk' I had to sit down because every bone in my body felt like jelly. I could not talk very clearly for several hours and had the most peaceful sleep that evening. Several years have passed since that experience, but I still hear the sound of heaven from time to time as I open my mouth to worship the Lord."

That same night several others had dramatic glory encounters as you will read in the following pages. This marked a major turning point for the two of us. For the first time in our lives the glory of the Lord began to be an experiential reality rather than a theological concept.

> "Going up and down among them were other forms that glowed like bright coals of fire or brilliant torches, and it was from these the lightning flashed. The living beings darted to and fro, swift as lightning."
> Ezekiel 1:13-14

After the meeting a group walked over to the pastor's home next door for coffee. One of the ladies in the parking lot came over to tell us that she had just seen a large bright angel following us as we walked. When we began to talk in the pastor's living room, we felt there was a sense that something "special" was up.

One of the first to speak was the pastor of The First Baptist Church in a nearby town. He began by saying that during the worship time he had one of the most unusual experiences he had ever had. He said he was caught up in the Spirit and taken into the heavenly realm. (Sound familiar?) The first thing he noticed was that he heard very loud music, but it wasn't like earthly music. To his ears it sounded like every song and note that had ever been played or sung was being sounded at the same time. In spite of the multiple layers of sound, he reported that the music had harmony and rhythm, but its most obvious characteristic was that it was loud.

He went on to say that as he was caught up into this realm he not only heard this incredible sound, but he also saw what appeared to be a ball of translucent light. Emanating from this ball of light were a vast array of colored points and flashes of lights. He described this glowing flashing orb in such vivid detail that we couldn't help but laugh because he was using such fluent and grand words. We had to stop and ask him occasionally what the word he was using meant. Another man spoke up and said that he, too had experienced a similar vision during worship that evening.

The pastor had barely completed his testimony of his remarkable experience when two of the teenage boys from the group burst through the flimsy screen door and into the heart of our conversation. They were pale, out of breath and both were talking rapidly at once. As we slowed them down and were able to understand what they were saying, we were left speechless by what they had to say.

The boys told us that they were walking up the dirt road from the meetinghouse to their home when something darted out from behind the vehicle parked in front of the house. They both saw the same thing at the same time (not a vision). They described it as a figure that had the shape of a man but couldn't have been a man because it moved so fast. The figure was glowing with a bright light and in their own words they both said, "It looked like lightning flashing back and forth in front of us." The being darted several times in this manner and then darted down the road away from them and disappeared. Then the boys turned to me and said, "What was it? Was it an angel or a demon?" Being the all-knowing, fully armed man of God for the hour, I stared blankly back at them and responded, "I dunno!"

But I determined that before daylight I would have an answer and I would get back to them. I asked the Lord to give me insight into what was happening before the next night's meeting so I could help these people (including myself) understand all that was happening among us and why. The first thing I did was to look up the word lightning in my Strong's Concordance. The first reference I turned to was, you guessed it, Ezekiel 1:13-14. This description fit perfectly what the boys had seen.

As I continued reading and meditating on what the pastor reported, I realized that what he had seen also matched in many ways the description of the things that the Prophet Ezekiel had described in Chapter 1:16-28. The culmination of this chapter is a record of Ezekiel's own glory encounter. Then it hit me—God was revealing His Glory. As a group we were being led into our own glory encounter.

The next day I was still meditating on what we were experiencing in "the compound," when I noticed a magazine among some literature in the pastor's office. It came from England and was the publication of a group there who called themselves "The Glory Folk." This group began in the 40's and continues to this day. Their distinctive has been the manifestations of the Holy Spirit that we have come to associate with revival. Their term for what we in the revival/renewal movement refer to as the manifestations is "the glory." Their understanding is that when the manifestations begin, the glory of the Lord is present.

The pieces of the puzzle were beginning to come together for me. God's glory really could be defined by "God showing up and bringing everything He has with Him." Visions, angelic encounters, laughter, falling under the weight of presence, miracles, signs and wonders are all manifestations of His glory. When His glory manifests anything can happen because we are talking about the actual presence of God being revealed in our midst.

Biblically I noticed a pattern to these glory encounters, or maybe I should more correctly say a purpose. The glory encounters we were experiencing that week together in a group setting and the scriptural accounts of the great men and women of God who had these same type encounters shared some common characteristics.

Glory encounters always involve a miraculous (supernatural) element. Signs, wonders, and miracles happen when God shows up. But these signs are not the glory; they just alert us to the fact that the glory of God is present. As God reveals himself, He *does* what He *is*. His nature is revealed in His glory, both His character and His power.

Perhaps most significantly for us, His Word is revealed. When He shows up, He speaks. Out of glory encounters come revelation upon which lifetimes of ministry and purpose are built. As Ezekiel encountered the glory of the Lord, God began to speak to Him concerning the fate of Israel and his call to the prophetic ministry. Ezekiel had a life altering experience. He was changed forever. The fate of a nation was wrapped up in that encounter. Nothing would ever be the same again. Glory encounters are transformational. We are a people who are being transformed by real life encounters with His tangible glory. Glory folk.

> "But we all, with open face beholding as in a glass the glory of the Lord, are changed into the same image from glory to glory, even as by the Spirit of the Lord."
>
> 2 Corinthians 3:18

SHOW ME YOUR GLORY

Moses had a personal encounter with God's glory. There was nothing theoretical or hypothetical about Moses' understanding of glory. He asked for it and He got it: a personal, tangible, life-changing encounter with the manifested glory of God.

> "And he said, My presence shall go with thee, and I will give thee rest. And he said unto him, If thy presence go not with me, carry us not up hence. For wherein shall it be known here that I and thy people have found grace in thy sight? is it not in that thou goest with us? so shall we be separated, I and thy people, from all the people that are upon the face of the earth. And the LORD said unto Moses, I will do this thing also that thou hast spoken: for thou hast found grace in my sight, and I know thee by name. And he said, I beseech thee, show me thy glory. And he said, I will make all my goodness pass before thee, and I will proclaim the name of the LORD before thee; and will be gracious to whom I will be gracious, and will

show mercy on whom I will show mercy. And he said, Thou canst not see my face: for there shall no man see me, and live. And the LORD said, Behold, there is a place by me, and thou shalt stand upon a rock: And it shall come to pass, while my glory passeth by, that I will put thee in a cleft of the rock, and will cover thee with my hand while I pass by: And I will take away mine hand, and thou shalt see my back parts: but my face shall not be seen."

Exodus 33:14-23 KJV

The revelatory encounter with God's glory began with a request. In the Kingdom of God, the principle is established for eternity—ask and you shall receive, seek and you shall find, knock and the door shall be opened to you. When you ask, be ready, because the encounter could be intense, personal and powerful—perhaps even frightening to some degree. Few people are prepared for the level of reality experienced when the glory of the Lord manifests. When God gets real, anything can happen and probably will.

Moses had a glory encounter. Peter, James and John had glory encounters (Matthew 17). Paul had a glory encounter that changed everything. He was knocked to the ground and nothing was the same when he got up. His purpose, direction in life, and even his name was changed (Acts 9). Remember the principle of the Kingdom? Ask, seek, knock. "Show me your glory, Lord."

When Moses boldly asked to see the glory (Ex. 33), God's response was, "OK, I will allow my goodness to pass before you." From this early encounter forward throughout scripture God's goodness and His glory are seen as synonymous. The terms are used interchangeably at times. As I mentioned earlier in the introduction, I asked the Lord to give me a definition of His glory that people could get hold of and really understand. I heard the Spirit of the Lord say, "The glory is when God shows up and brings everything He's got with Him."

> "How God anointed Jesus of Nazareth with the Holy Ghost and with power: who went about doing good, and healing all that were oppressed of the devil; for God was with him."
>
> Acts 10:38

Everywhere Jesus went He manifested the glory of the Father. The tangible expression of that glory is that good things happened. Everywhere Jesus went sick people were healed, demoniacs were delivered and provision was released. Nothing has changed. Everywhere Jesus shows up He manifests the glory of the Father. Miracles, signs, wonders and supernatural events happen when the presence of God is manifested.

The manifested glory of God is more than a mood or an atmosphere. His glory involves the tangible revelation of His goodness. When God shows up He brings the atmosphere of heaven with Him. The earthly realm is invaded by the heavenly, and God takes over. So another way of defining His glory is to say that it is when "God shows up and He takes over."

One of the most interesting miraculous events described in the ministry of Jesus is the transformation of water into wine at the wedding in Cana (John 2:1-11). The often-overlooked summary statement of that event says, "This beginning of miracles did Jesus in Cana of Galilee, and manifested forth his glory; and his disciples believed on him (John 2:11)." So, Jesus' miraculous act was specifically referred to as the manifestation of His glory.

When we use the term "doing good" in a modern religious context we are usually referring to a "good deed," some act of kindness done in the name of God—like feeding the hungry or clothing the poor or sheltering the homeless. All these are important, effective and mandated by scripture. But they are not what Jesus did when the Bible says, "He went about doing good." Every event or act of "goodness" on Jesus' part was miraculous in nature. Check it out for yourself. Examine scripture and see if you can find one example of Jesus doing something "good" that wasn't miraculous in nature. When we ask, as Moses did, that God show us His glory, we should expect to see His goodness manifested in tangible, identifiable, miraculous events.

When God shows up and brings everything He's got with Him—anything can happen. The atmosphere of heaven invades the human realm, which produces unexpected and even startling results, especially for those unaccustomed to the degree of reality that God is willing to reveal. Sometimes I find it amusing to hear people praying fervently for God to show up and then be taken totally off guard, even offended, by some of the things that happen when He actually does.

Seemingly the human body goes into something of an overload mode when His Glory manifests. Strange things can happen. People often shake or fall, simply overpowered by the experience. Tears are common, but so is laughter. The laughter is one of the more unexpected and puzzling results of His manifested glory for those who have a traditional rather than scriptural view of the atmosphere of heaven. Scripture says that in His presence is fullness of joy and at His right hand are pleasures for evermore.

> "Thou wilt show me the path of life: in thy presence is fullness of joy; at thy right hand there are pleasures forevermore."
>
> Psalm 16:11 KJV

Joy has a sound. It's called laughter. When God shows up, one of the things He brings with Him is joy. And real joy produces laughter. In many denominational churches, like the one I was brought up in, emotions and emotionalism were seen as highly undesirable (but only in a religious setting). Meetings in which tears or laughter or any strong emotion were evident were discouraged, if not outrightly forbidden. These outbursts were derisively referred to as "emotionalism."

After years of observing a varied number of responses to the presence of God, I have come to the conclusion that what is happening is not emotionalism in the purest sense. What is happening is a "spiritual" experience that has a profound effect on the emotions (as well as on the physical body). When the Holy Spirit moves on an individual, every component of our being is affected—mind, body, and soul. The encounter touches the emotions, but it is not emotional in origin. The distinction is important if you feel that emotions are entirely subjective and not "real" from a scientific, materialistic view. However, something very "real" is happening in a realm that touches the human heart like nothing else can and that has a remarkable outcome in the emotions.

After all, we are talking about an encounter where we are exposed to a level of the reality of the living God that few ever experience. People often faint, scream, shake or cry in the presence of rock stars or great leaders. How much more should that kind of response be expected in the presence of Almighty God, the Creator of the universe. When God gets real, so do we.

> "Whom having not seen, ye love; in whom, though now ye see him not, yet believing, ye rejoice with joy unspeakable and full of glory"
>
> 1 Peter 1:8

> "For it is the God who commanded light to shine out of darkness, who has shone in our hearts to give the light of the knowledge of the glory of God in the face of Jesus Christ."
>
> 2 Corinthians 4:6 KJV

The highest manifestation of the glory of God is seen in the face of Jesus Christ. According to 2 Corinthians 3:18:

> "But we all with unveiled face, beholding as in a mirror the glory of the Lord, are being transformed into the same image from glory to glory, just as by the Spirit of the Lord."

The Holy Spirit reveals the face of Jesus Christ. The outcome is that we are transformed into the image we behold—we shine!

In attempting to describe what a person experiences in a glory encounter, the best description seems to be that we are in an altered state. What is experienced is real, but in another realm from normal sensory perception. Jesus becomes so real that His tangible presence becomes the focus of all senses. We feel His touch, hear His voice, see His face, and smell His aroma—just as real and identifiable as sitting next to a lifelong friend and engaging them in normal conversation. But the encounter is on another level. We are usually not seeing with our natural eyes or hearing with our ears. Yet, we are hearing and seeing.

Recently I was listening to the radio when the host of the program signed off by saying, "I will see you tomorrow." Everyone listening knew we wouldn't "see" him with our eyes, and yet that is the only way to communicate the thought being expressed. "See you tomorrow" on the radio means we will hear his voice and experience his on-air personality audibly. In a similar manner, when we "see His glory" or "hear His voice" or "feel His presence" it is a real tangible experience that can only be conveyed in words that approximate the encounter. The encounter is so unique it defies description. But one thing is certain—when we see Jesus, we are transformed by the experience. And we are never the same again!

God is looking for those who are willing to embrace the full expression of His glory. A heart that is open to receive is the prerequisite. So, he Holy Spirit has defined the manifested glory of the Lord for me in the following terms: "When God shows up and brings everything He's got with Him!" Unfortunately, many choose to narrowly specify to God what they are willing to receive. The degree to which we are able to embrace the full expression of His glory will determine the extent to which we benefit from the encounter. His desire is to transform us from "glory to glory." He wants to take us to places we never dreamed we could go. But if we limit His access to our lives or limit our receptivity to the expressions of His glory that He chooses to use, we cut ourselves off from the changes that He desires to bring.

When God shows up in His glory, He is in control and we have lost control. He takes over. Our minds are affected—our thoughts, perceptions and senses are overloaded. Our physical bodies are often affected by the tangible manifestation of His glory; some shake, some fall, some laugh, some cry. Many experience a trancelike or dreamlike state. Some hear and/or see angels. Sometimes physical stuff happens. I have seen oil form on people's hands or "glory dust" appear and cover whole rooms and everything in them. Clouds, lights and sweet aromas have all been reported by those are caught up in His glory. Scripture says that the ultimate manifestation of the glory of the Lord is seen in the face of Jesus Christ.

When we see Jesus we have seen the ultimate expression of the glory of the Father revealed by the Holy Spirit. All the fullness of the Godhead dwelt bodily in Him. The assigned task of the Holy Spirit is to reveal Jesus to us, thus revealing the Father. When we see Jesus, we have seen the Father. We often opt for complexity when trying to express and experience all that God is, when what we really want is reality—the reality of Jesus. God with us. Somehow we mistakenly believe that in order for something to be significant and important it must also be complex. The truth is, the closer we get to Jesus, the clearer things become. Our minds become untangled, our thoughts become more cogent. Issues are suddenly resolved in a flash of divine revelation. Direction comes and decisions are easy. Even more astounding—circumstances change, physical healing takes place and provision miraculously materializes. Freedom and emotional healing come. The manifested presence of Jesus brings joy and peace like no other experience can, and it changes us in ways that defy description.

> "Ye men of Israel, hear these words; Jesus of Nazareth, a man approved of God among you by miracles and wonders and signs, which God did by him in the midst of you, as ye yourselves also know" Acts 2:22 KJV

> "How God anointed Jesus of Nazareth with the Holy Ghost and with power: who went about doing good, and healing all that were

> oppressed of the devil; for God was with him." Acts 10:38
>
> "This beginning of miracles did Jesus in Cana of Galilee, and manifested forth his glory; and his disciples believed on him."
>
> John 2:11

Several key terms are used in the verses above that are intertwined and have a direct impact on experiencing and understanding the glory of the Lord. In Jesus dwelt the fullness of the Godhead bodily. When we see Jesus we are seeing the glory of the Father revealed.

In that revelation comes the demonstration of the goodness of the Father. Everywhere Jesus shows up good things happen. As Moses asked to see the glory, God said I will show you my goodness. So Jesus reveals the true nature and character of the Father by revealing His goodness.

In Jesus' ministry, this goodness takes the form of the miraculous. Miracles are the acts of goodness that Jesus did which scripture says, "Manifested forth His glory." If you examine what Jesus actually did as described in the Gospels you will fail to find one single act of "goodness" that did not involve the miraculous.

Signs and wonders are God's way of getting our attention and saying, "Hey, something is going on here, you need to pay attention." The signs and wonders themselves are not the focal point, instead they are used to draw our focus to what God is saying and doing.

The burning bush with Moses and the star that guided the Magi to the newborn Jesus are both examples of signs and wonders that served to get somebody's attention so that they could hear what God was saying or take notice of what He was doing. The bush caused Moses to turn aside and hear the voice of God. The star led the Magi to Jesus. Once the star got them to Jesus, its purpose had been served. The significant event was Jesus; the star was simply God's way of getting them to where they needed to be. On the day that Solomon's Temple was dedicated, the day was marked by the visitation of God's glory. The visitation also included the appearance of smoke that filled the building as well as the priest being overcome by His presence and being rendered unable to stand.

I have seen God use a number of signs, wonders and miracles to draw attention to what He is saying and doing in my life. I have seen manifestations of oil, feathers and unusual displays of light. I have lost count of the number of healing miracles, as well as miracles of provision, that I have witnessed. I believe that we will see even more displays of God's unlimited creative ability as we draw closer to the end of the age. God is good.

Many signs and wonder are associated with the manifestation of the glory, but the focus is on seeing and hearing the voice of God through the presence of Jesus Christ. Miracles happen because that is what Jesus does when He gets real. The tangible manifested Glory of the Lord is all about Jesus getting real and revealing who He really is. He is living proof that God is good.

A dynamic involved in an encounter with the glory of God is that of it always producing change. Most often the change is radical. A persecutor of the faith named Saul goes forth zealously pursuing Christians for the express purpose of killing them hoping to wipe out what he considers to be a rapidly spreading heresy. He comes out with a changed named, as a follower of Jesus Christ and an apostle of the group he was trying to wipe out. Radical change.

> "Now the Lord is that Spirit: and where the Spirit of the Lord is, there is liberty. But we all, with open face beholding as in a glass the glory of the Lord, are changed into the same image from glory to glory, even as by the Spirit of the Lord."
> 2 Corinthians 3:17-18

Changed - ***metamorphoō*** (Gk.)

Thayer Definition:

> 1) To change into another form, to transform, to transfigure
>
> 1a) Christ appearance was changed and was resplendent with divine brightness on the mount of transfiguration

We must understand the dynamic of how this radical change occurs so that we, too, can experience the transformation of ever-increasing glory. First, we are told in 2 Corinthians 3:17 that the Lord is the Spirit. The work of the Holy Spirit is never to be relegated to some less than essential element of the Christian experience. The Holy Spirit is the Spirit of the Living God. The Holy Spirit is God's presence in man. We are told in Colossians 1:27 that , "Christ in us is the hope of glory." The anointed one, Christ, and His anointing in us is our hope of the revelation of the true Glory of the Lord. Without the work of the Holy Spirit we cannot experience the Glory of the Lord.

There is no competition in Heaven. The Father, Son and Holy Spirit are in perfect harmony and unity. One heart, one mind, one purpose; the Godhead moves, acts and speaks as one. Jesus said, "If you have seen me you have seen the Father." He goes on to say that He is sending "another." His work is clearly outlined in John 16. In this widely misinterpreted and misapplied passage Jesus makes it clear that the Holy Spirit has come to reveal the glory by passing on what the Son has received from the Father.

> "Howbeit when he, the Spirit of truth, is come, he will guide you into all truth: for he shall not speak of himself; but whatsoever he shall hear, that shall he speak: and he will show you things to come. He shall glorify me: for he shall receive of mine, and shall show it unto you. All things that the Father hath are mine: therefore said I, that he shall take of mine, and shall show it unto you."
>
> John 16:13-15 KJV

As we continue in 2 Corinthians we see that we are "beholding" the Glory of the Lord "as in a glass" or "through a mirror." In other words, we see the Glory, but it's not like we see normally. We are seeing through Jesus as revealed by the Holy Spirit.

Seeing Jesus for who He really is results in change. We are transformed into the image we see. The change is not just a one time experience or encounter. It is described as being "from glory to glory." This is a continuing transformational process that produces in us the character, nature and mind of Christ.

When we see Jesus the savior, we are saved. When we see Jesus the healer, we are healed. When we see Jesus the provider, provision manifests. Even more incredibly, we see that the Holy Spirit working in and through us can lead others to this same saving, healing, providing knowledge.

As if to make sure there is no mistake about it, the passage in 2 Corinthians ends with these words, "By the Spirit of the Lord." The revelatory work that produces this transformation is the work of the Holy Spirit.

GLORY IS THE GOAL

> "For all have sinned, and come short
> of the glory of God"
>
> Romans 3:23

This verse is seen as the definitive description of the biblical view of sin. The word sin (*hamartano*-gk) literally means "to miss or fall short of the mark." Then to underscore the meaning, "*hustereo*" is used which also means "to fall short." The word picture is of an archer who is aiming for a bulls-eye but the arrow falls short of the intended target.

The part of this scripture that caught my attention recently is not the falling short portion, but the goal itself. Like many others my attention has been on the definition of sin. I think that speaks volumes. The Church's focus has been on sin. Whether abstinence *from* sin or participation *in* sin, the focus has still been the same: sin. If we follow the principle that we become like what we focus on the most, then it is inevitable that as we remain preoccupied with the topic of sin, it will dominate our behavior.

What caught my attention recently is the goal. The goal that is held up as the standard is "the glory of God." Sin is falling short of "the glory." His glory is the goal, not just the minimum conduct required to be acceptable.

For some time now I have been defining "glory" as when God shows up and brings everything He's got with Him! The manifested Glory of the Lord is His presence, His Kingdom and His demonstrations revealed. His Glory is His nature, character and power on display.

When we see that Glory is the goal, our view of sin is radically altered. What we are shooting for in our personal lives, as well as our corporate gatherings, is the reality of His manifested Glory shining through these earthen vessels.

We are not merely seeking the highest expressions of behavior modification and human will power; our goal is to reveal the true presence, nature, character and power of God. That's not hard, THAT'S IMPOSSIBLE!! Only by His Glory working in us can we express His Glory. We have to receive it to display it.

The time has come that we raise the bar. Sin is not just what we don't do, the behavior we avoid. Sin is the failure to actively display all that God is. We may not hit the mark every time, but if we are not even shooting for that mark, we will surely never hit it. If we focus on the true goal, His Glory, we break the cycle of preoccupation with sin. We also get the focus off of our own inadequacy and begin to seek His fullness. Even if we don't hit the mark every time, at least we will hit it some of the time. Obviously, without the Holy Spirit working in us to impart His glory, we can never achieve the goal set before us. That is the reason Paul said; "This I say then, Walk in the Spirit, and ye shall not fulfill the lust of the flesh (Gal. 5:16)."

THE COVENANT OF GOODNESS

"I will gather them out of all countries, whither I have driven them in mine anger, and in my fury, and in great wrath; and I will bring them again unto this place, and I will cause them to dwell safely: And they shall be my people, and I will be their God: And I will give them one heart, and one way, that they may fear me forever, for the good of them, and of their children after them: And I will make an everlasting covenant with them, that I will not turn away from them, to do them good; but I will put my fear in their

> hearts, that they shall not depart from me. Yea, I will rejoice over them to do them good, and I will plant them in this land assuredly with my whole heart and with my whole soul. For thus saith the LORD; Like as I have brought all this great evil upon this people, so will I bring upon them all the good that I have promised them."
>
> Jeremiah 32:37-42

God's intention is to have a people set aside for one express purpose and that is to reveal His glory in the earth. In order for that to have full expression, a people must willing to be recipients of his goodness. In Jeremiah 32, God speaks of the day and the people coming that will be marked by an everlasting covenant that is established to do them good. This people will have a heart knowledge rather than a head knowledge of God. They will also be marked by a reverential awe of God that produces obedience from the heart. But what will be most striking about this covenant is that God will be actively, even aggressively "doing them good."

Acts 10:38 tells the story of how "God anointed Jesus...who went about doing good and healing all those oppressed of the devil." The New Covenant precisely fits the prophetic description of Jeremiah of this coming covenant of goodness.

> "For the earth shall be filled with the knowledge of the glory of the LORD, as the waters cover the sea."
>
> Habakkuk 2:14

The knowledge of the tangible, observable, manifested Glory of the Lord will fill the earth. That glory will be demonstrated and put on display through a covenant people who are a demonstration of the goodness of God "in the land of the living." David cried out for the goodness of God in the land of the living. That is the promise of God to us and the innate yearning in every believer's heart imparted by the Holy Spirit.

> "I had fainted, unless I had believed to see the goodness of the LORD in the land of the living."
>
> Psalm 27:13

The land of the living"—you know—where you live, at your house, in your body, in your family, in your bank account, at your job—the reality of Jesus manifested in the real world. That is our inheritance and our heart's cry! His glory manifest in our lives and the result is changes in everyday practical situations. The goodness on display reveals the true nature of the living and loving God who desires a people to bless. He rejoices to do us good. It is not a bother or an imposition, it is His revealed will and intention to be a good Father to His sons and daughters.

THE REVIVAL CONNECTION

> "To the intent that now unto the principalities and powers in heavenly places might be known by the church the manifold wisdom of God."
> Ephesians 3:10

The Church of Jesus Christ fully functioning, fully empowered, filled with His Glory on display for all to see—that is Gods intention for His people. The modern expression of the Church in most western nations falls so short of that goal that it would appear to be impossible to achieve. As we say in Texas, "You can't get there from here."

With men it is impossible, but with God all things are possible. A group of 500 people witnessed Jesus ascension back to the heavenly throne. He told them to go to Jerusalem and wait for the coming of the Holy Spirit. Of that group, one hundred and twenty showed up for the meeting. They were obediently gathered in the upper room on the Jewish feast day of Pentecost when the promise came. A glory encounter miraculously transformed one hundred and twenty people that day. A rag tag group of religious, political and social misfits, scarred and scared by the rejection of friends and family and the execution of their leader, suddenly became a group of united, bold witnesses who turned the world upside down with their message and its wonder working power.

The most startling change was in their leader Peter. He had denied Jesus and gone back to fishing. Apparently he comprehended very little of what He had witnessed in the previous three years as he and the twelve had followed Jesus day after day. He still was confused and filled with shame at his own personal failure and the incongruities of Jesus' earthly ministry. Suddenly, this fear-filled failure rose and boldly addressed over 5000 people to clearly and unequivocally declare that what they were seeing was the fulfillment of the words of the prophet Joel and the promise of Jesus that the Holy Spirit would be poured out on mankind. It's almost as if you could her Peter exclaim; "OH! NOW I GET IT! This IS that spoken by the prophet..."

The change was not just a revelatory internal change. Not only did the knowledge come but it came with power! The one hundred and twenty now not only spoke words that testified to the transformational work in their own hearts, they also now carried the same authority and power that Jesus had displayed to heal the sick and deliver those in bondage. The Church was born in a Glory Encounter that revealed Jesus through a group of people by the work of the Holy Spirit. My belief is that revival is the restorative work of the Holy Spirit to bring a carnal and fallen Church back to that same transformational encounter to produce the same results of the day of Pentecost – today!

GOLD

> "But as it is written, Eye hath not seen, nor ear heard, neither have entered into the heart of man, the things which God hath prepared for them that love him. But God hath revealed them unto us by his Spirit: for the Spirit searcheth all things, yea, the deep things of God."
> 1Corinthians 2:9-10 KJV

Have you ever experienced an extended dry season? For me, it was about 1998. Nothing seemed to be happening. The tremendous rush of progress and blessing that flowed into my life following a revival encounter in 1993 seemed to have run its course. I thought maybe revival was over for me. It sure seemed that way. I prayed. I put it honestly to God. If what I had already seen and heard in the early days of the '90s was all that was available, then I would be happy and content for the rest of my life with what I had already experienced. Most people live their whole lives and, at best, see one or two mighty moves of God. Many leaders from the past have gone happily to their reward having only witnessed one true revival in their lifetime and books and stories are still being written about their lives. I would certainly praise Him for the multiple outpourings I have witnessed during my lifetime.

However, something wouldn't let me adopt that posture. I just felt there should be more. What the prophets had spoken concerning the great revival to come certainly seemed to point to more than what I had already witnessed. Somehow the Spirit of God within me was drawing me on in spite of my dryness of soul. Then I began to hear reports, mainly from a friend of mine from South Africa, that something new was beginning to happen in the meetings he was conducting. The joy of the Lord that was such a hallmark of the move we had experienced in '93 was still in evidence, but a new wave of signs was being released as well. To be specific, gold was "happening."

A close and respected friend reported to me that gold colored dust was appearing on people in his meetings. In some cases people's dental work was turning gold. Increased healing miracles and miracles of provision were also breaking out. I was greatly encouraged by his reports and others I began to hear about a fresh release of the anointing. I started to seek the Lord and ask Him for this same release in my life. I have discovered a principle of the Kingdom. God doesn't show partiality. If one of His children has received something from Him, then it is available to all of His children. Rather than be jealous about what He is doing in someone else's ministry and grumble and murmur about my own condition, I rejoice because I know that if He is doing something for them then the same thing is available for me. I ask for it.

The answer didn't come instantly, but when it came, boy did it really shake things up in my life! In the months following my initial seeking of God in this matter, I really began to understand the concept of "eye hath not seen." The fresh release of anointing and the new levels of Glory that began to flow into my life were things I couldn't have asked for because I didn't even know they were available. Most significantly, I discovered that not only was God not through yet, He had only just begun. And the best was yet to come!

The testimonies that I was hearing about gold dust (glory dust) and gold teeth accompanied by dramatic healing and provision were a great encouragement to me after the extended period of drought I had been experiencing. I remember several times when I was preaching during the high point of revival for me, from '93 to '97, that I would often say I'd rather be driving a truck than go back to dead religion. Well, sure enough, God gave me that opportunity. In 1998 I got so dry I started driving a truck and waiting to see what happened next. As I heard these new reports towards the end of that year, I began to seek the face of God again about revival.

Some friends in ministry were gathering at my home on Sunday afternoons in those days. We all began to pray and ask God for a fresh anointing and these new manifestations. One of my prophetic friends had a word about the gold at one of those home meetings and an admonition to pray one more time. We did, and we went one more step; we actually began to look in each other's mouths to see if there were any "dental miracles." Sure enough, my friend's wife had what looked like a filling that was gold in color and in the shape of a cross. Several others that day reported fillings that changed colors or glory dust on their skin or clothing. My wife, Carol, said her mouth had "that dentist office taste."

One of the women with small children had to leave early before we prayed. I knew she would be interested so I called her on the phone the next day about what had happened and suggested she might check her own teeth. She said she would and hung up the phone. In just a matter of seconds the phone rang and it was her. I could tell she was very excited. She breathlessly explained to me that just a couple of weeks before the Sunday meeting she had taken her oldest son to the dentist for four fillings. After she hung up the phone, she had checked his mouth first. He didn't have any gold fillings—HE DIDN'T HAVE ANY FILLINGS AT ALL! The fillings that the dentist had put in just a few weeks before were gone, and where they had been, were perfectly whole teeth.

Now this really got my attention. I was beginning to get breathlessly excited myself. I started sharing with everyone I knew what we had seen. That's when things started to multiply. Seemingly, every time we started talking about these unusual signs and wonders they manifested. On the phone, in conversations, in meetings, whatever the setting—the gold manifested.

> "The silver is mine, and the gold is mine, saith the LORD of hosts."
> Haggai 2:8 KJV

Because I first heard of the gold manifestations from a good friend of mine, I wasn't as skeptical of the reliability of the reports as I normally would have been. I was even more encouraged when I heard that the gold teeth had also been reported in some meetings at the Toronto Airport Christian Fellowship. As with all new things I hear about, I had two basic questions: Is it You, Lord? & What are You saying?

Again the Lord led me to my old reliable friend, The Strong's Exhaustive Concordance. I looked up references to gold and for some reason I was particularly drawn to Haggai 2:8 where the scripture says, "The silver is mine, and the gold is mine, saith the Lord of Hosts." That settled that issue for me. If the Bible says it is His, then that is all I needed to know.

The second question, however, is where it got really interesting for me. When God uses dramatic signs and wonders it is to get our attention. He usually wants to get our attention so that we will focus on what He is saying or doing. Again, the burning bush is a good example. Because Moses turned aside and looked at the bush that was burning but not consumed, God spoke to Him. The revelation that came from that encounter provided Moses with a map for the rest of His life and for the destiny of the Jewish people. And another good example is the Star of Bethlehem. The star was not the focus. The star led the Magi to Jesus. Jesus was the focus; the star was simply God's sign to get them where they needed to be to worship the newborn King of Kings. Dramatic signs, wonders and miracles are to get our attention so that we will focus on what God is saying and doing.

> "Ye men of Israel, hear these words;
> Jesus of Nazareth, a man approved
> [attested, NKJV] of God among you
> by miracles and wonders and signs,
> which God did by him in the midst
> of you, as ye yourselves also know."
> Acts 2:22 KJV

I wanted to know the significance of the gold manifestations prophetically. Too often people treat very significant events that are happening in the Body of Christ as if they were just a passing fad for their entertainment. When this happens the full impact of what God wants to accomplish is lost. Instead of seeking God in the manifestation, immature believers often focus on the manifestation and fail to recognize the real importance of what they are experiencing. Like Peter on the Mount of Transfiguration (Matt.17: 3-5), they want to build a monument to the occasion as a memorial to their participation rather than understand the true meaning of the moment. It is interesting that on that occasion God himself spoke unequivocally and said; "This is my Son in whom I am well pleased, listen to Him!" The message was: FOCUS ON JESUS—LISTEN TO HIM!!

The prophet Haggai was sent by God to stir the people to return to work on the rebuilding of the Temple. During the restoration period after Israel's return from the Babylonian captivity, the people had grown weary and discouraged. In their malaise they turned aside from their destiny and purpose and began to focus on their own houses. This led to the condition described in the first chapter of Haggai where the people were living in paneled houses while the Temple was in a state of total neglect. Haggai's call and admonition was for the people to return to their destiny and true calling. God was not finished with His house!

As I began to meditate on Haggai I realized that in the context of the answer to my first question: Was the gold manifestation of God? came the answer to my second question as well: What are you saying, Lord?. It hit me like a brick. The condition of Israel paralleled my own condition and the condition of many whom I knew in the Body of Christ. Revival had come. We had gotten off to a great start. However, opposition came. The work was difficult and often our motives were questioned. The continual back-pressure and the vehement opposition from those in the Church had greatly hindered the work of revival. Because of my own feelings of personal rejection, I had shut down. Like Peter who returned to fishing, I drove a truck. The effect in my life was perfectly described by the prophet.

"Thus speaketh the LORD of hosts, saying, This people say, The time is not come, the time that the LORD's house should be built. Then came the word of the LORD by Haggai the prophet, saying, Is it time for you, O ye, to dwell in your ceiled houses, and this house lie waste? Now therefore thus saith the LORD of hosts; Consider your ways. Ye have sown much, and bring in little; ye eat, but ye have not enough; ye drink, but ye are not filled with drink; ye clothe you, but there is none warm; and he that earneth wages earneth wages to put it into a bag with holes. Thus saith the LORD of hosts; Consider your ways. Go up to the mountain, and bring wood, and build the house; and I will take pleasure in it, and I will be glorified, saith the LORD. Ye looked for much, and, lo, it came to little; and when ye brought it home, I did blow upon it. Why? saith the LORD of hosts. Because of mine house that is waste, and ye run every man unto his own house."

Haggai 1:2-9 KJV

I heard clearly the implication of my dry condition. I had given up and quit. As a result, I was suffering. It was time to return. God started something and He wasn't finished yet. Revival was not then, nor is it now, over. God is building His house and His city, and He has called us to that destiny. The time is here for the Church to return to her calling and destiny.

In the message of the prophet Haggai, God clearly declares His plan for Israel emerging from slavery in Babylon to their destiny in the land. The first priority was establishing a city, Jerusalem, and then rebuilding the Temple. The message to the people was that the project they were involved in needed completion. His promise to them was that the provisions necessary were available and that He was capable of equipping them for the task. They were working in the shadow of the former Temple built by Solomon. Its chief characteristic was that it was practically gold and silver-plated. Haggai assures the people that God has got the gold. The job can be done, now is the time and they are the people.

> "For thus saith the LORD of hosts;
> Yet once, it is a little while, and I will
> shake the heavens, and the earth,
> and the sea, and the dry land; And I
> will shake all nations, and the desire
> of all nations shall come: and I will
> fill this house with glory, saith the
> LORD of hosts. The silver is mine,
> and the gold is mine, saith the

> LORD of hosts. The glory of this latter house shall be greater than of the former, saith the LORD of hosts: and in this place will I give peace, saith the LORD of hosts."

Haggai 2:6-9 KJV

In reading Haggai 2:6, I realized that the prophet had hit the fast forward button. He was no longer talking to a people long ago. He was talking to a generation who would see their whole world shaken. He was talking to a generation who would see an unprecedented worldwide revival break out. He was talking to our generation.

> "See that ye refuse not him that speaketh. For if they escaped not who refused him that spake on earth, much more shall not we escape, if we turn away from him that speaketh from heaven: Whose voice then shook the earth: but now he hath promised, saying, Yet once more I shake not the earth only, but also heaven. And this word, Yet once more, signifieth the removing of those things that are shaken, as of things that are made, that those things which cannot be shaken may remain. Wherefore we receiving a kingdom which cannot be moved, let

> us have grace, whereby we may serve God acceptably with reverence and godly fear: For our God is a consuming fire."

Hebrews 12:25-29 KJV

"The glory of the latter house"—those words jumped off the page. We are being built into a house—His House and a Temple–His temple. Not only are we being built into a dwelling place for His glory, but that glory (the latter house glory) is going to exceed anything and everything He has ever done up to that point. What an incredible time we live in.

> "We are laborers together with God: ye are God's husbandry, ye are God's building. According to the grace of God which is given unto me, as a wise masterbuilder, I have laid the foundation, and another buildeth thereon. But let every man take heed how he buildeth thereupon. For other foundation can no man lay than that is laid, which is Jesus Christ. Now if any man build upon this foundation gold, silver, precious stones, wood, hay, stubble; Every man's work shall be made manifest: for the day shall declare it, because it shall be revealed by fire; and the fire

shall try every man's work of what sort it is. If any man's work abide which he hath built thereupon, he shall receive a reward. If any man's work shall be burned, he shall suffer loss: but he himself shall be saved; yet so as by fire. Know ye not that ye are the temple of God, and that the Spirit of God dwelleth in you? If any man defile the temple of God, him shall God destroy; for the temple of God is holy, which temple ye are."
1Corinthians 3:9-17 KJV

"And are built upon the foundation of the apostles and prophets, Jesus Christ himself being the chief corner stone; In whom all the building fitly framed together groweth unto a holy temple in the Lord: In whom ye also are builded together for a habitation of God through the Spirit."
Ephesians 2:20-22 KJV

"Ye also, as lively stones, are built up a spiritual house, an holy priesthood, to offer up spiritual sacrifices, acceptable to God by Jesus Christ. Wherefore also it is contained in the scripture, Behold, I lay in Zion a chief corner stone, elect, precious:

and he that believeth on him shall not be confounded. Unto you therefore which believe he is precious: but unto them which be disobedient, the stone which the builders disallowed, the same is made the head of the corner, And a stone of stumbling, and a rock of offense, even to them which stumble at the word, being disobedient: whereunto also they were appointed. But ye are a chosen generation, a royal priesthood, a holy nation, a peculiar people; that ye should show forth the praises of him who hath called you out of darkness into his marvelous light: Which in time past were not a people, but are now the people of God: which had not obtained mercy, but now have obtained mercy."
1Peter 2:5-10 KJV

MEANWHILE, BACK AT THE RANCH

"And they overcame him by the blood of the Lamb, and by the word of their testimony; and they loved

not their lives unto the death."
Revelation 12:11

The understanding of the prophetic significance of the gold manifestation found in Haggai emboldened me as I continued to share with others what we were seeing. The more we talked about the gold, the more it happened. I noticed something else happening almost immediately. Everywhere the gold manifested it increased faith to receive miracles of healing and provision.

What began with that small group in my living room on a Sunday afternoon began to quickly spread as I determined to share with everyone I knew what was happening. That decision led me back into the calling of God on my life to revival ministry. It also led me back to "deepest darkest" East Texas where God had begun to teach me about His Glory several years before. I picked up where I left off.

For years a group of pastors had been meeting weekly in the small lumber town of Kirbyville, Texas. Long before it was fashionable, their simple goal was to pray for revival in their community. They were a diverse group – Baptist, Methodist, Pentecostal and Independent Charismatic – meeting each week for breakfast and then prayer. I had gotten to know most of them several years earlier during a round of revival meetings at "the compound."

I followed the leading of the Spirit to drive down from Fort Worth just for their meeting and to share what had happened in my living room a few weeks earlier. As we gathered in his office, the pastor of First Baptist Church turned to the other men and told them I had something to share, and then he turned the meeting over to me. I told them about the gold manifestations, the young man who had received the dental miracle, and the connection I saw with the prophecies of Haggai.

As I finished speaking I was wondering what their reaction was going to be. These men had a wonderful fellowship, but they were from a wide spectrum theologically. The pastor of First Baptist broke the silence. He said simply, "Well, would you pray for us?" Would I? You bet I would! I led them to pray a simple prayer that I have since led thousands to pray with me: "Lord, we are Your Temple; Lord, I am Your Temple; fill Your Temple with Your glory—now."

I handed one of the pastors a flashlight and encouraged him to check out the teeth of those gathered. A nervous laughter spread through the group. I could tell this was a bit of a stretch for some of these men of God. But sure enough, the first man checked had gold fillings. The pastor with the flashlight exclaimed to the others, "They are turning gold right now." All the inhibitions and religious protocol went out the window. Like a group of curious little boys, we crowded around this one poor guy's opened mouth to watch in amazement as his dental work turned gold right in front of our eyes.

Several of the men reported changes in their dental work that day. It was a Wednesday so most of them had midweek services that night. As they shared in their churches, reports began immediately of more gold teeth. The move was on!

> "But Peter, standing up with the eleven, lifted up his voice, and said unto them, Ye men of Judea, and all ye that dwell at Jerusalem, be this known unto you, and hearken to my words: For these are not drunken, as ye suppose, seeing it is but the third hour of the day. But this is that which was spoken by the prophet Joel; And it shall come to pass in the last days, saith God, I will pour out of my Spirit upon all flesh: and your sons and your daughters shall prophesy, and your young men shall see visions, and your old men shall dream dreams: And on my servants and on my handmaidens I will pour out in those days of my Spirit; and they shall prophesy: And I will show wonders in heaven above, and signs in the earth beneath; blood, and fire, and vapor of smoke: The sun shall be turned into darkness, and the moon into blood, before that great

and notable day of the Lord come:
And it shall come to pass, that
whosoever shall call on the name of
the Lord shall be saved."

Acts 2:14-21 KJV

As the reports of gold teeth and glory dust began to spread through the piney woods of deep East Texas, so did revival fire. The first Wednesday night after the pastor's meeting in Kirbyville several of the fellowships involved reported outbreaks of dental miracles, healing and other unusual signs.

The men of God leading the churches were not unprepared for revival. Several had been experiencing a move of God for a number of years. They were eager and hungry for this fresh outbreak. Two groups in particular, The New Covenant Fellowship of Jasper and Bonami Missionary Baptist Church of Kirbyville, were already conducting joint Sunday night services. I was invited to share at one of these services.

It was a small building, that would hold one hundred if completely full, and it was packed with over one hundred people. Most of those present had already heard about the gold and had come to see what God would do next. He didn't disappoint us. God showed up in His glory. His tangible presence was as thick as the 100% humidity in the air. The air-conditioning and the sound system were overloaded as God's people joined in worship with a country flavor.

When I say God showed up in His glory, this is what I mean. His multidimensional nature was on full display. Several reported being saved, others returned to the Lord in this atmosphere of love and forgiveness. Many were instantly healed of serious illnesses and conditions. We heard numerous reports of unusual signs and wonders. Some who had been adamantly opposed to the manifestations of the Holy Spirit were powerfully filled and began to have manifestations of their own. The unity of the Spirit in the bond of love was the order of the day. As men of God opened their arms to receive each other and what was happening in their midst, congregational distinctions melted with the summer heat, and we merged into one people, the people of God.

It was evident to all that we were in the midst of a fresh outpouring of the Holy Spirit in revival. The meetings were extended to the weeknights and continued for several weeks. In the next section I will detail more of the remarkable miracles we witnessed in Jesus' name. But first let me point out the direct connection between signs, wonders, miracles and revival. What began with the gold teeth, the Holy Spirit multiplied into a full blown revival in just a matter of days. The message that came forth was right out of Haggai. God was building His Temple (us) and filling it with His Glory (Him), and we were experiencing the results—His goodness on display (salvation, restoration, unity, miracles, signs and wonders) in the "land of the living" real world.

> "And I, brethren, when I came to you, came not with excellency of speech or of wisdom, declaring unto you the testimony of God. For I determined not to know any thing among you, save Jesus Christ, and him crucified. And I was with you in weakness, and in fear, and in much trembling. And my speech and my preaching was not with enticing words of man's wisdom, but in demonstration of the Spirit and of power: That your faith should not stand in the wisdom of men, but in the power of God."
>
> 1 Corinthians 2:1-5

This revival was happening in the most unlikely place among the least likely people. We were in a rural setting in an area of Texas that most people don't even know exists. The church that was hosting the meetings was a part of a Baptist denomination that didn't fellowship with other Baptists, much less Pentecostals, Charismatics, or Methodists. But here we were night after night coming together in unity in His presence to experience the manifestations of His glory.

One of the remarkable things I observed from the beginning of the gold manifestations was how quickly the sign spread when people talked about it. The more they talked the more it happened. And I am not talking about some contrived manipulative verbal ambush, just regular everyday conversations would lead to reports of gold fillings or glory dust showing up. Distance seemed to be no barrier either as there were several reports of people talking on the phone and someone on the other end seeing an immediate manifestation.

In this atmosphere of miracles, many came for healing. Jesus, The Healer, manifested in a remarkable way. One of the first was a man healed of lung cancer who had already had one lung removed. The doctors said he had only days left. His health was restored and he lived several more years after these meetings. The pastor of the host church was healed of palsy that he had carried since childhood. A man confined to a wheel chair for over a year, paralyzed with no feeling or movement below the waist, received both feeling and movement in one of the meetings.

One night during a time of powerful release, a lady got up out of her seat and made her way to the aisle. I motioned for her to come forward. She obediently came to the front. As I laid my hand on her forehead, she fell to the floor immediately and began to speak in tongues. Her Baptist pastor came over to me and jokingly said that he would have gladly paid me $100 for that one. When I asked why, he said that this woman had been very vocal in her criticism of what was happening and didn't want any part of it. The next night when she came in the building her whole countenance had changed. She was laughing and singing and praising God. Later in the service, I asked her to come and share with the congregation what had happened. As she testified, the truth came out. I had totally misread the situation. She wasn't getting up to come and receive prayer. She was trying to make her way to the bathroom. She just didn't want to embarrass herself so when I called her forward she came. But the Holy Spirit did His work anyway. She was full of thanksgiving for the immediate joy and peace that flooded her as she received the fullness of the Baptism of the Spirit. In a Glory encounter sometimes even your enemies become your friends.

> "But as many as received him, to them gave he power to become the sons of God, even to them that believe on his name: Which were born, not of blood, nor of the will of the flesh, nor of the will of man, but of God."   John 1:12-13

> "He said unto them, Have ye received the Holy Ghost since ye believed? And they said unto him, We have not so much as heard whether there be any Holy Ghost." Acts 19:2 KJV

I am frequently asked, "What is the key to revival?" It would be impossible to nail it down to one thing. Unfortunately, many have tried to produce a plan or procedure to follow to insure instant revival. They never work. Revival is a sovereign work of God in the hearts of man. However, there is one common denominator I have observed anywhere true revival breaks out and His glory is manifested.

During the '90's I had the opportunity, as many others did, to go to the places where powerful moves of God had broken out. I was in several Rodney Howard-Browne meetings in a number of locations. I visited Toronto twice for a week each time and Brownsville Assembly of God in Pensacola, Florida for a week. This was along with the meetings that I was holding during the same period where many of the same things were occurring.

I asked the Lord what these diverse ministries had in common that released the Glory in revival. The answer came very simply; they all said *yes*. When God showed up and the Spirit began to move the leaders and the people involved had the same response. In spite of their theological, sociological and stylistic differences they all said *yes*. And not a grudging, I guess it will be ok, kind of *yes*; but an emphatic aggressive enthusiastic *YES*!!

The Holy Spirit will show up wherever He is invited (sometime even where He is not invited), but He will remain where He is celebrated rather than merely tolerated. Being in the traveling ministry I am often the guest in homes and churches. Some people go out of their way to show true hospitality and gladly receive you. On those occasions I feel welcome and want to stay. Others are barely able to conceal their feelings of imposition through thinly veiled politeness. I am sure you have had the same experience as you have been a guest in someone's home. It doesn't take long to know if you are really welcome or just being tolerated.

Many have had a one time or brief exposure to revival. The Father in His mercy and sovereignty will pour out His Spirit in revival glory anywhere people are gathered in His name. Where He makes His habitation instead of just a visitation is where people make room for Him and allow Him to have His way.

Ultimately, one of the central issues faced in revival is control. When God shows up for real, He expects to be treated like God. He is funny about that. When God shows up in His manifested tangible Glory, He takes over. It is no longer our plans and preferences that matter, but we are being led, directed and empowered by the very presence of the living God.

Have you received the Holy Spirit since you believed? Don't be too quick to answer. I mean have you fully embraced Him as the presence of the living God and accepted the complete array of all that He is capable and eager to do? Having had a taste of what that reality is like, are you eager for more? Have you settled in your heart the issue of whether you really want Him or are you still a bit embarrassed about what happens when He really gets hold of people and has His way? Have you really received Him?

Chapter 2
He Is Building A House

> "For thus saith the LORD of hosts; Yet once, it is a little while, and I will shake the heavens, and the earth, and the sea, and the dry land; And I will shake all nations, and the desire of all nations shall come: and I will fill this house with glory, saith the LORD of hosts. The silver is mine, and the gold is mine, saith the LORD of hosts. The glory of this latter house shall be greater than of the former, saith the LORD of hosts: and in this place will I give peace, saith the LORD of hosts."
>
> Haggai 2:6-9 KJV

As in the days of Nehemiah, Ezra, Haggai and Zechariah, God is involved in a massive building project. He is building a city and a temple. Jerusalem was to be rebuilt as a prosperous city of peace. The city was to be a place where the nations could interact with and observe God's blessing on His chosen people. Jerusalem was to be a place of commerce, society and protection from enemies.

In the midst of the people, at the heart of all they did, was to be a structure, the Temple, which was at the same time the symbol and the reality of God's abiding presence. In the same way Moses spoke with God about leading the Israelites into the land of promise; the first issue that was dealt with was God's abiding presence. Both Moses and God agreed that there was nothing to distinguish Israel from all the other nations on the earth unless the presence of the Lord was with them. Moses went so far as to say that he was not going unless God was going with them. What is the distinguishing characteristic of His Church that is to separate us from all the other institutions, religions, ethnic groups, social organizations and humanistic philosophies? *Immanuel*, God is with us.

Most modern day moves of God seem to be comprised of two distinct phases. First, there is the initial outpouring. During this phase a spontaneity and dependency on the presence of God is prevalent. Usually this is a time of unknown men being used in powerful ways that challenge the old established order of things. The focus is on personal experience, rather than institutions and organizations. As things progress, a gradual shifting into the second phase occurs that includes more focus on organization, plans, buildings and financial stability. Unfortunately, this shift is often accompanied by the loss of vision and purpose that birthed the move in the beginning stages.

Surprisingly, I don't find scriptural reason to resist the shift itself. However, I do believe the transition is often a move from operating in the Spirit in the first phase to attempting to carrying out the vision in the flesh in the second phase. The result is simply that old, cold, dead institutions built on the traditions of men are replaced by new, cold, dead institutions built on updated technologically and slick methodology which are simply enhanced versions of the same old, tired traditions of men.

Without question, the necessity for human accessibility to the presence of God is needed. He wants His glory to be observable and the benefits clearly verifiable. This requires human contact and visible displays of blessings. Provision, abundance, health and other signs of well-being and security are not in opposition to the purposes and plans of God, rather they are a validation and confirmation of His goodness. However, when man takes over in manipulative, greedy, materialistic pride, God's glory is replaced by the glory of human achievement. Inevitably, what results in the latter case is so far inferior to what God had planned that it can only be described as sinful.

First, a place must be established for His permanent abiding presence so that the personal reality of His glory is continually manifested in open displays of His goodness. Then, an equally significant place is to be established in which human interaction and social activity take place with the abiding presence of God as the context for community life. Having begun in the Spirit, will we be perfected in the flesh? No, but too often that is the methodology applied by the Church. Both the Temple and the City are to be built according to the purpose, plans and power of the Builder and filled with His abiding presence.

> "For he looked for a city which hath foundations, whose builder and maker is God."
>
> Hebrews 11:10

Let me make this a little less esoteric and more down to earth. When Carol and I were dating in the early 1970s, we were invited to hear a speaker who was going to be at a place called the "Shepherd's Inn" in East Texas. We were involved in the local version of the Jesus Movement in those days and were always looking for a place where God would "show up."

We weren't disappointed that night. Although we had never heard of him and had no idea who he was (he was a lot older than most of the crowd), we were blessed by the power and reality of the teaching and the depth of understanding of the Word of God this man displayed. There were maybe 30 or 40 present at the most, but in those days we considered that a pretty good size meeting. The speaker's name? Kenneth Hagin.

As most of you who are reading this know, Pop Hagin established a school, publishing, radio and TV ministries that grew enormously and remain today as a legacy to the faith movement that he pioneered. In the early days of his long ministry, the life, revelation, and glory were present, just as in the latter years. The ministries that Brother Hagin established later became the occasion for millions of people worldwide to be exposed to what began simply as revelation in his heart.

> "For the earth shall be filled with the knowledge of the glory of the LORD, as the waters cover the sea."
> Habakkuk 2:14

God's plan is to have a people in which His glory resides as a permanent habitation. This people will be blessed with supernatural, tangible evidence of the presence of God. His nature and character will be their nature and character. His miracle working power will be on display through signs wonders and miracles done at the hands of His servants. His goodness will be their never-ending inheritance.

This people will be a direct fulfillment of the promise made to Abraham that in his seed all the peoples of the earth would be blessed. His Spirit will flow through this people and be a river of healing to the nations to fulfill the words of the prophet Elijah.

This people will be the Body of Christ fully functioning, fully equipped and Holy unto Him. This people will be transformed by the work of the Holy Spirit into the image of Jesus Christ. This people who were not a people will be made into a Temple not made with human hands but are the workmanship of God almighty. They will be a dwelling place of His Glory for all the nations of the earth to behold.

The glory of this Latter House will cause the nations of the earth to come to the desire of all nations. As the heavens and earth shake and kingdoms and nations fall, that which cannot be shaken shall remain. In the midst of great darkness a great light will once again shine. And the nations of the earth will be drawn to its shining—a city set on a hill that cannot be hidden, a people filled with the glory of the Lord; King Jesus.

Can this be? Is it possible? Will the glory of this latter house really exceed the glory of the former?

> "Then he answered and spoke unto me, saying, This is the word of the LORD unto Zerubbabel, saying, Not by might, nor by power, but by my spirit, saith the LORD of hosts."
> Zechariah 4:6 KJV

"Know ye not that ye are the temple of God, and that the Spirit of God dwelleth in you?"
1Corinthians 3:16 KJV

"What? know ye not that your body is the temple of the Holy Ghost which is in you, which ye have of God, and ye are not your own?"
1Corinthians 6:19 KJV

"And what agreement hath the temple of God with idols? for ye are the temple of the living God; as God hath said, I will dwell in them, and walk in them; and I will be their God, and they shall be my people."
2 Corinthians 6:16 KJV

"Now therefore ye are no more strangers and foreigners, but fellow citizens with the saints, and of the household of God"
Ephesians 2:19 KJV

"Ye also, as lively stones, are built up a spiritual house, an holy priesthood, to offer up spiritual sacrifices,

acceptable to God by Jesus Christ."
1Peter 2:5 KJV

Something I've noted among many Christians is their tendency to believe that for something to be significant or important it has to happen to somebody else somewhere else at some other time. Great encounters with God—miracles, signs, and wonders –always seem to happen to someone special in some unusual locale. "After all, if it were really important how could it be happening to me? If God wanted to do something significant, this would be the last place he'd choose." Seems so humble, doesn't it? But it is false humility. In 2 Corinthians 4:7, Paul specifically says that God has chosen to reveal His glory in earthen vessels so that the power is obviously from Him and not us. The real question is: "If not now, when? If not here, where? If not you, who?"

When it comes to great faith, one of the most difficult and often hidden issues of the heart has nothing to do with our belief in God's ability. His sufficiency is indisputable, accepted without question. The real issue is often, "But can God do it through me?" Believing that God can use you, that is where real faith comes in. We are the people, the city and the house. In the New Testament there is no doubt concerning the true nature of the coming Temple. We are it. *You* are it!

If the knowledge of the glory of the Lord, the tangible manifested Glory of God, is going to fill the earth, then guess where He will show up in your town. That's right, it'll have to be through you. If you are a believer then you are the vessel that God has chosen to pour His Glory into. Let me ask you a question about where you live; is it on a map? Is it in the earth? Then guess what, His glory is going to be revealed through His Temple where you live. That means you are the one responsible for revealing His Glory where you live.

King David cried out to God to see the glory of the Lord in the 'land of the living.' The land of the living: at your house, on your job, in your family, in your bank account, at your address. "Father, we are your Temple. Fill Your Temple with your glory. Lord, I am your Temple. Fill your Temple with your Glory, NOW!"

IT ISN'T FINISHED

> "Thus saith the LORD of hosts; Consider your ways. Go up to the mountain, and bring wood, and build the house; and I will take pleasure in it, and I will be glorified, saith the LORD."
>
> Haggai 1:7-8 KJV

After the meetings in East Texas in spring of 1999, the renewed work spread to other locations in Texas: Weatherford, Granbury, Clyde, and Sweetwater. What I saw happening led me to the conclusion that the prophetic mission and message of Haggai was equally important today in the Body of Christ as it was when spoken to the people of Israel. I saw that the gifts and callings of God poured out in the atmosphere of revival, and glory encounters are without repentance. The anointing doesn't go away, we do. More than once I heard Pastor John Arnott of the Airport Christian Fellowship in Toronto say that if you believe revival is over, then unfortunately for you, it is.

As I ministered in one outbreak after another beginning in 1999 through the summer of 2000, I soon realized that I had totally misread the heart of God. Revival wasn't over. The lifestyle of walking in the Spirit of God is to be a progressive "glory to glory" experience. He has called us to an end-time work, and He is not finished with that work. Though many who initially experienced the outpouring of the Holy Spirit in revival have moved on to other things, God has not completed the purpose for which He poured out His River; the healing of the nations.

In Weatherford we had a series of spontaneous unplanned meetings that extended for four months. Night after night the glory manifested. Dramatic healing miracles were reported from conditions such as sleep apnea, post-polio syndrome, cancer and hepatitis-C. Hundreds of people reported normal amalgam fillings in their teeth turning gold. Many told of visions, dreams and dramatic revelatory encounters. The local and national news media caught wind of the event and published numerous newspaper articles from San Diego to Houston to Boston.

We were featured on live call-in secular radio broadcasts in several major markets. The CBS-TV affiliate in Dallas did a feature story on the revival including a live satellite feed from the parking lot on the night the story aired. All this happened with no advertising, just spreading the story by word of mouth. Most importantly for me, night after night lost men and women, young and old, found Jesus. Those who had fallen away from their first love were restored in an atmosphere of forgiveness and joy.

The experience of one youth group sums it up for me. They had come from the nearby city of Granbury to Weatherford to be in the meetings. The group witnessed the "glory dust" and had some powerful personal encounters with the Holy Spirit. They returned from the meetings and were back in their regular high school environment the next day. The Pastor's wife from their church just happened to be substitute teaching in one of the classes that day. At the end of the day's lesson she allowed them to talk quietly among themselves. Several of the teenagers from the group started excitedly telling others what had happened in the meetings.

Because of the educational guidelines, the teacher couldn't join in the conversations, but she listened with interest as they talked about seeing the gold dust and being overcome by the power of the Holy Spirit. Sure enough, the gold began to manifest right there in the high school classroom.

One young man was listening intently. He was not in the Church group. In fact he was a hard core "Goth" dressed in black from head to toe. He approached the teacher and began to talk. Surprisingly he told her that he believed that this really was from God. However, he added he knew that God would never do something like that (the gold dust manifestation) for "someone like me." Since the young man initiated the conversation the pastor's wife now felt free to talk with him. She pointedly said, "I believe he would." The young man protested and again expressed his doubt that God would do something for someone who had messed up as badly as he had. Finally, the teacher couldn't contain herself any longer. She called his name and said, "I know He would because you are covered in gold right now." The young man looked at his clothing for the first time and realized that he, too, was covered in what looked like multicolored glitter from head to toe.

The story doesn't stop there. By God's providence the meetings closed out in Weatherford and another series of meetings quickly began in Granbury in the same church that this youth group was from. The "Goth" came to the meetings with the youth group and was saved. He brought his family. Brothers and sisters were saved. Finally his mother and father came and were saved, too. They were separated at the time and decided to get back together. And as if to top it all off with a heavenly exclamation mark, the father was healed of cancer.

Wherever I travel I find people who have been touched by the power of God and then gone on to experience rejection, disappointment or failure. Like the Israelites of Haggai's generation, they discovered the purposes and plans that God has for His people have enemies. Unfortunately, those enemies can be as readily found on the inside of the Church as on the outside "in the world." Wounds are inevitable. Hurts come. The resulting feelings and experiences have left thousands immobilized and neutralized in a state of introspection, or worse, despair and depression. Some are overtaken by overt sin, others simply by ambivalence.God's word to you is "I'M NOT FINISHED WITH YOU YET!" Right now He is calling you back to your destiny in His plan.

One final point from the experience of the Israelites on this subject really excites me. He doesn't wait until the house is finished to bless those who return to the work. In Haggai 2:16-19 we can see clearly that from the moment you return to His calling and destiny on your life, the blessings of His presence begins to flow.

> "Consider now from this day and upward, from the four and twentieth day of the ninth month, even from the day that the foundation of the LORD's temple was laid, consider it. Is the seed yet in the barn? yea, as yet the vine, and the fig tree, and the pomegranate, and the olive tree, hath not brought forth: from this day will I bless you." Haggai 2:18-19 KJV

IT'S GOING TO LOOK LIKE HIM

"Now if any man build upon this foundation gold, silver, precious stones, wood, hay, stubble; Every man's work shall be made manifest: for the day shall declare it, because it shall be revealed by fire; and the fire shall try every man's work of what sort it is. If any man's work abide which he hath built thereupon, he shall receive a reward. If any man's work shall be burned, he shall suffer loss: but he himself shall be saved; yet so as by fire. Know ye not that ye are the temple of God, and that the Spirit of God dwelleth in you? If any man defile the temple of God, him shall God destroy; for the temple of God is holy, which temple ye are."
1Corinthians 3:12-17 KJV

God is building His house. "There is no other foundation that can be laid than that which is laid, which is Jesus Christ." After the foundation of the revelation of Jesus is laid, then we have a choice. What are we going to use to construct this building?

Wood, hay and stubble are still used as ingredients for building material in certain regions of the world. We have a name for the buildings constructed in this manner. They are called mud huts. Straw is mixed with mud and walls go up. Maybe it covers the need for basic shelter, but it's certainly not a temple. It may be what everyone else is building, but it is still a mud hut. It may be an elaborate design, but it's still a mud hut. It may be the biggest in the village, but it's still a mud hut. Gold, silver, precious stones speak of a Temple— a Temple fit to contain the glory of The King. We choose.

A few years ago I met a very interesting man who worked with marble. His specialty was counter tops and bathtubs. He took me to his warehouse where he kept the marble stored until time to craft it into whatever he was making. He was especially proud of several large wooden shipping crates that contained very special marble from Israel known as Jerusalem marble. He explained to me that this was very valuable not only because of it rarity but also because of the way it was extracted.

One of the most desirable characteristics in marble is that consistent patterns and colors run through the stone so that when it is assembled in the final use it matches from one piece to the next. In order for this consistency to be present the stone slabs have to be cut in the quarry from the same vein of marble, preferably at the same time and then packed and numbered together so that the slabs are as close to a perfect match as possible.

As I was listening to this skilled artisan describe this process, I realized something about the Temple that God is building in us. Jesus is the cornerstone, the first piece that sets the pattern and standard for the rest of the structure. The Father wants the building to match. He wants it to look like Jesus throughout. From start to finish, He desires that the materials match. Anywhere you look in the building, you should see Jesus.

> "Unless the Lord builds the house,
> They labor in vain who build it;
> Unless the Lord guards the city, The watchman stays awake in vain."
> Psalm 127:1

IT'S THE ANOINTING THAT MAKES THE DIFFERENCE

> "Now the Lord is that Spirit: and where the Spirit of the Lord is, there is liberty. But we all, with open face beholding as in a glass the glory of the Lord, are changed into the same image from glory to glory, even as by the Spirit of the Lord."
>
> 2Co 3:17-18

Comparing the current condition of the Church in much of the western world to the prophecy of the latter house glory in Haggai, an honest assessment would have to say, "You can't get there from here." But that fails to take into account what God says through the prophet Zechariah.

> "Then he answered and spoke unto me, saying, This is the word of the LORD unto Zerubbabel, saying, Not by might, nor by power, but by my spirit, saith the LORD of hosts."
> Zechariah 4:6 KJV

The glory of the Lord poured out in His people will be a work of the Holy Spirit, not of men. Only a transformational work of the presence of God can bring about the degree of change required for the Church, The Temple of God, to reflect and reveal His true nature, character and power. Through the revelatory work of the Holy Spirit, we will be transformed into the image we are beholding, the glory of the Lord in the face of Jesus Christ. This move of God on His people will not be the result of methodology, technique, style, technology, or education. It will not be earned, deserved, or achieved—it will be received.

A very good friend of mine, Steve, loves to say, "It's the anointing that makes the difference." Several years ago he went to Mexico on a ministry trip. The pastor that took Steve on the trip also was acting as his interpreter. They reached a city on the western coast of Mexico where they were scheduled to minister in a small church for just one service. The guide/interpreter had double booked for the

Sunday, so he was speaking in another church at the same time. He left Steve to speak in this city alone with no interpreter and no one in the congregation that spoke English. Steve's Spanish skills were limited to a few phrases he had learned by listening to preaching and interpreters in his own meetings. He knew *"fuego"* (fire), *"venga Espiritu Santo"* (come Holy Spirit) and *"Gloria"* (glory) and that was about it.

He felt impressed of the Lord just to get up and say the words he knew. So he just began repeating the phrases he knew in Spanish. In just a few minutes the Holy Spirit fell on the people and the fire of God broke out—shouting, laughing, people falling under the power of God. But here it is in Steve's own words:

> "They had assigned an 'interruptator' for me but she was really struggling with my English. Plus, she was trying to interpret to Spanish and then the tribal language, Ixtepec, which it turned out, was for most of the audience. If my memory serves me correctly, the presence of God was so very thick, and the interpreter was struggling, and I **KNEW WHAT GOD WAS ABOUT TO DO**, so I just began saying very emphatically, "La presencia de Dios está aquí, ahorita!!" Over and over with strong

emphasis on RIGHT NOW—THIS MINUTE, "AHORITA —ESTE MINUTO," and it was like a glory bomb went off. That whole place was overtaken by God's presence. I laid my hands on about half-a-dozen people and turned them loose to do the same. Bodies were laid out all over that building. The pastor's wife was standing up whole rows of people, laying her hands on the first in the row, and down they all went—shaking, vibrating, crying, laughing. It was awesome. God is awesome!"

When the meeting was over Steve left almost immediately for his next engagement.

Three or four years went by and Steve never heard anymore from that fellowship. I invited him to go with me on a trip to Mexico with another friend, Daniel. Daniel had arranged us to be in this same city that Steve had visited several years before. As we were driving to the church he told us the story and wondered out loud if it might be the same church he had been in on that first trip. Sure enough, as we pulled up to the Pastor's home he recognized it as the same place. When we were greeted at the front door by the Pastor's wife she excitedly exclaimed, "Esteban! (Steve!)" She began to rapidly tell us of a dream she had three nights earlier where she saw him coming with us back to their church. She had not known he was on the trip with our group. Finally, she got to the most amazing part of the story for me. She said that their church had never been the same since that Sunday when Steve first ministered. The visitation of the Holy Spirit that day was so strong that it sparked a revival that completely transformed their small struggling group into a vibrant growing fellowship. Language barriers, human limitations, no matter what barriers exist—God is able! ARISE, SHINE!

> "Arise, shine; for thy light is come,
> and the glory of the LORD is risen
> upon thee."
>
> Isaiah 60:1 KJV

As we behold Jesus, we are transformed into His likeness by the work of the Holy Spirit. Because it is the glory of the Lord that is revealed in the face of Jesus Christ we are transformed into a vessel of His glory. We shine with the imparted glory of the Lord. It is not possible to remain passive after encountering the manifested glory of God. An extreme reality requires an extreme reaction.

INTENSITY

Several years ago, I was ministering in an Assembly of God Church in San Diego, CA. It was on a Sunday night, and I was preaching on the subject of the glory of the Lord. As I was preaching I began to get an impression from the Lord of a very large bonfire built around the city. I am from Texas, and what I saw was something similar to the huge structurally engineered bonfire built every year by the students of Texas A&M before the annual football rivalry with University of Texas. It is an assembly of telephone pole size logs constructed specifically for the purpose of making an impressive fire. In the vision I saw this fire igniting into a ring of glory that engulfed the city of San Diego.

As I was preaching this message, there was a group of about fourteen youth seated close to the front of the auditorium. To me they seemed to be very restless. They were on the edge of their seats nervously shifting around occasionally whispering to one another. Being the "discerning great and mighty man of God for the hour," I again totally misjudged the situation. I thought they were anxious for me to get through so that they could get outside and do the important teenager stuff, like talk on their cell phones. Boy, was I wrong.

What I didn't know was that these kids had just returned from a trip to Pensacola, Florida, where they had attended revival services at Brownsville Assembly of God. As I was talking about the glory, they knew exactly what I was talking about and were just in a hurry for me to get the preaching out of the way so they could get in the zone. I finally finished and gave the altar call for those who wanted to receive the glory. All fourteen of the group jumped from their seats and ran to the front.

As they ran to the altar I realized my mistake and in a flash of true discernment heard the heart of God. The Spirit spoke to me, "I want to meet them with the same intensity they have come to meet me." A Holy Ghost bomb exploded in my chest. I jumped from the platform and shouted at the top of my lungs "FIRE!" As soon as the sounds left my lips the group instantly and violently were thrown to the floor by the power of God. All went down immediately without me ever touching them. For the remainder of the night into the early hours of the next morning those kids remained on the floor under the power of the Holy Spirit with shouting and "joy unspeakable and full of Glory." I have never forgotten those words that I heard in the Spirit that night: "I want to meet them with the same intensity they have come to meet me." God is still looking for people whose hearts are passionately turned towards Him, seeking His face. He wants to meet you with the same passion and desire that you are directing towards Him.

"WE ARE YOUR TEMPLE..."

I believe that we have totally underestimated the importance and commonality of glory encounters as they relate to the experience of normal New Testament Christianity. Whatever name you choose to give it, the early Christians were first led into a supernatural, personal, revelatory experience with the Holy Spirit through the name of Jesus Christ. That experience became the foundation for everything else that happened in their lives from that point forward.

> "Grace and peace be multiplied to you in the knowledge of God and of Jesus Christ our Lord, as His divine power has given to us all things that pertain to life and godliness, through the knowledge of Him who called us by glory and virtue, by which have been given to us exceedingly great and precious promises, that through these you may be partakers of the divine nature, having escaped the corruption that is in the world through lust."
>
> 2 Peter 1:2-4

The epistles of the New Testament were written by the Apostles as letters back to people that already had the bond of a common experience. They were written for the purpose of growth and edification in that experience. In contrast, much of the efforts of modern Christianity is to use the epistles as requirements on how to achieve the results that were present from the very beginning of the walk during the early days of the Church. We are trying to educate people into an experience while in the Early Church, the Apostles and Evangelists released the power and led the people into the experience first. The early believers had the advantage of the inner working of personal revelation from the Father from the start of their walk, rather than trying to derive understanding through human logic and reason, as is most often the case today.

The reason many modern Christians fail to experience the glory of the Lord is that they are trying desperately to earn the right to this encounter through diligent study, human knowledge or formulas and procedures followed in the flesh. In the Acts Church the darkest sinners had a supernatural encounter with the glory of the Lord first. The transformation produced an immediate effect. Those early uneducated and unqualified believers began to immediately operate in the gifts of the Holy Spirit. They had more understanding and power than most modern believers possess after a lifetime of study and preparation for a graduation and commencement type event that never occurs.

It was a common experience of the Holy Spirit that gave them unity.

> "Endeavoring to keep the unity of
> the Spirit in the bond of peace."
> Ephesians 4:3

It was the common experience that gave them revelation.

> "And Jesus answered and said unto
> him, Blessed art thou, Simon Bar-
> jona: for flesh and blood hath not
> revealed it unto thee, but my Father
> which is in heaven."
>
> Mat 16:17 KJV

It was the common experience that gave them power.

> " But ye shall receive power, after that the Holy Ghost is come upon you: and ye shall be witnesses unto me both in Jerusalem, and in all Judea, and in Samaria, and unto the uttermost part of the earth."
>
> Acts 1:8 KJV

It was the common experience that became the theological standard by which all new experiences and issues were settled.

> " And as I began to speak, the Holy Ghost fell on them, as on us at the beginning. Then remembered I the word of the Lord, how that he said, John indeed baptized with water; but ye shall be baptized with the Holy Ghost. Forasmuch then as God gave them the like gift as he did unto us, who believed on the Lord Jesus Christ; what was I, that I could withstand God? When they heard these things, they held their peace, and glorified God, saying, Then hath God also to the Gentiles granted repentance unto life."
>
> Acts 11:15-18 KJV

If our goal now is to recapture the life, love, power and purity of the New Testament Church, then I believe we must personally and corporately begin to flow in the "glory to glory" experiential and revelatory realm that was the foundation of the Early Church. That's what I call revival!

Chapter 3
Fellowship of the Mystery

WARNING: CONTAINS HUMOR

> "To me who am less than the least of all the saints, this grace was given, that I should preach among the Gentiles the unsearchable riches of Christ. And to make all see what is the fellowship of the mystery, which from the beginning of the ages has been hidden in God who created all things through Jesus Christ; to the intent that now the manifold wisdom of God might be made known by the church to the principalities and powers in the heavenly places according to the eternal purpose which He accomplished in Christ Jesus our Lord, in whom we have boldness and access with confidence through faith in Him"
>
> Ephesians 3:8-12

I am starting a new secret society. Handshakes and all. This clandestine organization is already at work. Meetings are held regularly. As word gets out, everyone will want to find out about this group. Its name? The Fellowship of the Mystery. I've actually suggested to some that they rename their Churches. Under the Fellowship of the Mystery banner, interest in the community will certainly be raised. Everyone will want to know the secret. The news media might even enquire: "What's the mystery?" At least it is a biblical name—it is in the Bible—which is more than can be said for many church names.

The Apostle Paul's use of this term is not accidental and perhaps a bit overlooked. He is revealing a reality hidden from the beginning of time. He goes so far as to say that the hidden revelation is THE eternal purpose of God. That's big stuff!

The incarnation, Jesus Christ, is the great mystery now being revealed. Jesus lived, walked, spoke and acted out of the reality of God's purpose. The amazing part of this mystery is that the depth, width and breadth of it is still being revealed. That's where the 'fellowship' part comes in. The multifaceted, multidimensional wisdom of the Father is now being made known BY THE CHURCH! That's you and me. He is using us to reveal His wisdom to everyone who is watching. And guess who is watching— EVERYONE! All of creation is watching. Angels, demons, the heavenly hosts, humanity, animals, plants and even the rocks are watching (to see if they have to take our place in crying out). See Romans 8:19-22 for confirmation.

We are called and chosen, in current lingo 'tasked,' with the purpose of revealing His glory to all who are watching, and everyone has their eyes on the church. It's time to shine. Carol had a word while we were in Brisbane. She saw the people of God under a camouflage tarp like the military uses. The people were armed with powerful weapons designed to bring mass destruction to the enemies' tactics. As she watched, the tarp was removed and the people came out of hiding to take their place in overcoming the enemy. In this unveiling, everyone was suddenly aware of the mighty weapons in the hands of the believers as the hidden came out in the open. I believe that is the word for the hour.

THE MYSTERY EXPOSED

> "...but there is a God in heaven who reveals mysteries..."
>
> Daniel 2:28

> "And he said unto them, 'Unto you it is given to know the mystery of the kingdom of God: but unto them that are without, all these things are done in parables.'"
>
> Mark 4:11

"Now to Him who is able to establish you according to my gospel and the preaching of Jesus Christ, according to the revelation of the mystery kept secret since the world began but now made manifest, and by the prophetic scriptures made known to all nations, according to the commandment of the everlasting God, for obedience to the faith—to God alone wise, be glory through Jesus Christ forever, Amen."

Romans 16:2-27

"But we speak the wisdom of God in a mystery, even the hidden wisdom, which God ordained before the world unto our glory..."

1 Corinthians 2:7

"This is how one should regard us, as servants of Christ and stewards of the mysteries of God."

1 Corinthians 4:1

"...that I should preach among the Gentiles the unsearchable riches of

Christ; And to make all men see what is the fellowship of the mystery, which from the beginning of the world hath been hid in God, who created all things by Jesus Christ: to the intent that now unto the principalities and powers in the heavenly places might be known by the church the manifold wisdom of God, according to the eternal purpose which he purposed in Christ Jesus our Lord: In whom we have boldness and access with confidence by the faith of him."

Ephesians 3:9-12

"Whereof I am made a minister, according to the dispensation of God which is given to me for you, to fulfill the word of God; even the mystery which hath been hid from ages and from generation, but now is made manifest to His saints; to whom God would make know what is the riches of the glory of this mystery among the Gentiles; which is Christ in you, the hope of glory..."

Colossians 1:25-26

In the garden, Adam and Eve had the opportunity to continue in unhindered fellowship with the Father in a completely satisfied state of existence. Only through the promise of something "secret" and superior were they enticed to fall. They were led to believe that they could achieve what they already had. In much the same manner, people today spend their lives searching for something that is already available through Jesus Christ.

The false promise made with the suggestion that Eve eat of the tree of the Knowledge of Good and Evil is that she would obtain special insight enabling her to become "like God." Ever since, man has been attempting to ascend to the throne of God by enlightenment that achieves some form of "self-actualization." Every major world religion at its core promotes man's attempt to achieve a godlike status through intense and intricate self-effort.

Modern literature and cinema is filled with countless examples of fiction based on this theme. Especially interesting are the novels of Dan Brown who seeks to capitalize on the shady surroundings and dark activities of groups who profess to hold the secrets of this mystery. The problem with Brown's books is that they don't go far enough in unmasking the true nature of the groups he seeks to expose. He settles for half-baked theories to provide his audience with cheap chills and thrills. As is most often the case, truth is stranger, more despicable and more destructive than fiction.

From the beginning of human history the enticement of the enemy to his victims is to find a secret hidden mystery that takes man to godhood. As Satan himself aspired to ascend to and usurp the throne of the Most High, he apparently operated under the notion that he can amass a great following and take over by storm. Even more sinister is the probability that in the failure that came through his own rebellion, Satan saw the impossibility of success so that now his goal is to steal as many of God's creation as possible and take them with him to ultimate destruction. Much like the demented scorned lover of so many fictional tales, Satan seeks to steal, kill and destroy that which is most precious to the One he cannot control or supplant.

As with any deception, there has to be a bit of truth to make it plausible. The enemy's lie is not a 180 degree opposite of God's truth, rather it is about two degrees off point—just enough to divert you from your true destination and end up lost in a wilderness of confusion. At the heart of every mystery cult is the lie that they alone possess the secrets of human divinity and the accompanying power. The members of the mystery cults are seen as the true guardians of the truths that must be passed on and entrusted to the special ones who submit to their requirements. Much intrigue and deception surround these groups and, yes, some do seek world domination through their 'enlightenment.'

Much like the Masons exercised almost complete political and economic control over Southern culture in the USA for several generations, these groups seek to maintain dominion for their own personal gain and the achievement of there ultimate goals in the arts, entertainment, business, government, education and even in the institutional church. Many, if not most, of those involved are oblivious to the evil core of the groups with whom they have identified. Deceived themselves, they believe that they are on the true path to ultimate human enlightenment and fulfillment. They believe they are pursuing God, rather than the perverted entity to whom they are, in reality, subservient.

A mystery does exist. The Truth behind the divine mystery is more fantastic and otherworldly than any fiction can imagine. The revelation of this mystery does lead to our becoming 'sons of God'(Galatians 3:26). The life or death, heaven or hell, all important distinction is that the genuine key to 'enlightenment' does not find itself in human effort or wisdom. The mystery is revealed in Jesus Christ. Faith in Him and in Him alone brings the revelation of the mystery which is now made known to all. The work is His from beginning to end. We are the beneficiaries of His grace and mercy. His ultimate goal is to redeem man from the curse of sin and death and restore the unhindered fellowship that the loving Father had with His children.

We now have access to the glory of the Father through the blood of Jesus Christ. The realization of God's redemptive plan is completed with the glorification of His children when we truly are transformed into "the same image" that we behold in the revelation of His glory in the face of Jesus Christ. This work is accomplished by the work of the Holy Spirit in us today and in finality at His ultimate appearing (2 Corinthians 3 & 4). The hidden purpose of God that is now exposed was revealed by Jesus on the cross, in His resurrection and in His reign. The completion of God's full disclosure will be in the visible return of Christ and the establishment of the new heaven and new earth.

The Church of Jesus Christ is the steward of this mystery today and its task is the propagation of the revelation of this mystery. The truth that is better than any fiction is that God has prepared a container for His glory both now and for eternity. That container (vessel) is His people, The Church. The Church of Jesus Christ is the dwelling place of God. We are His temple and His body, the embodiment of the Godhead in the earth today! Just as "the fulness of the Godhead dwelt bodily in Him [Jesus]," His glory now resides in the Church through the indwelling presence of the Holy Spirit. The Church is on display for all of creation to behold the glory of the Lord in His temple. A temple 'not made with human hands'—not a building—but a people called and gathered for His eternal purpose of revealing His true nature and power.

Paul said that the preaching of the cross was to the Jews a stumbling block and to the Greeks, foolishness. They just didn't get it. It is a mystery on full display, hidden in plain sight, uncloaked by God but unseen by the masses. "Open our eyes Lord, we want to see Jesus."

THE LATTER HOUSE GLORY

In the message of the prophet Haggai, was a clear declaration of God's plan for Israel. Emerging from slavery in Babylon to their destiny in the land, the first priority was establishing a city, Jerusalem, and rebuilding the Temple. The message was simple; finish the project. God's promise was that the necessary provision was available and that He was capable of equipping them for the task.

They were working in the shadow of the former Temple built by Solomon. Its chief characteristic was that it was practically gold and silver-plated. Haggai assures the people that God has the gold and the silver. The job can be done. Now is the time and they are the people.

"For thus saith the LORD of hosts;
Yet once, it is a little while, and I will
shake the heavens, and the earth,
and the sea, and the dry land; And I
will shake all nations, and the desire
of all nations shall come: and I will
fill this house with glory, saith the
LORD of hosts. The silver is mine,
and the gold is mine, saith the
LORD of hosts. The glory of this
latter house shall be greater than of
the former, saith the LORD of hosts:

and in this place will I give peace, saith the LORD of hosts."

Haggai 2:6-9 KJV

"See that ye refuse not him that speaketh. For if they escaped not who refused him that spake on earth, much more shall not we escape, if we turn away from him that speaketh from heaven: Whose voice then shook the earth: but now he hath promised, saying, Yet once more I shake not the earth only, but also heaven. And this word, Yet once more, signifieth the removing of those things that are shaken, as of things that are made, that those things which cannot be shaken may remain. Wherefore we receiving a kingdom which cannot be moved, let us have grace, whereby we may serve God acceptably with reverence and godly fear: For our God is a consuming fire."

Hebrews 12:25-29 KJV

In reading Haggai 2:6 I realized that the prophet had hit the fast forward button. He was no longer talking to a people long ago. He was talking to a generation who would see their whole world shaken. He was talking to a generation who would see an unprecedented worldwide revival break out. He was talking to us.

"The glory of the latter house," those words jumped off the page. We are being built into a house—His House—and a Temple—His temple. Not only are we being built into a dwelling place for His Glory, but that Glory (the latter house glory) is going to exceed anything and everything He has ever done up to that point. What an incredible time we live in.

> "For we are laborers together with God: ye are God's husbandry, ye are God's building. According to the grace of God which is given unto me, as a wise masterbuilder, I have laid the foundation, and another buildeth thereon. But let every man take heed how he buildeth thereupon. For other foundation can no man lay than that is laid, which is Jesus Christ. Now if any man build upon this foundation gold, silver, precious stones, wood, hay, stubble; Every man's work shall be made manifest: for the day shall declare it, because it shall be revealed by fire; and the fire shall try every man's work of what sort it is. If any man's work abide which he hath built thereupon, he shall receive a reward.

If any man's work shall be burned, he shall suffer loss: but he himself shall be saved; yet so as by fire. Know ye not that ye are the temple of God, and that the Spirit of God dwelleth in you? If any man defile the temple of God, him shall God destroy; for the temple of God is holy, which temple ye are."

1Corinthians 3:9-17 KJV

"And are built upon the foundation of the apostles and prophets, Jesus Christ himself being the chief corner stone; In whom all the building fitly framed together groweth unto a holy temple in the Lord: In whom ye also are builded together for a habitation of God through the Spirit."
Ephesians 2:20-22 KJV

"Ye also, as lively stones, are built up a spiritual house, an holy priesthood, to offer up spiritual sacrifices, acceptable to God by Jesus Christ. Wherefore also it is contained in the scripture, Behold, I lay in Zion a chief corner stone, elect, precious: and he that believeth on him shall not be confounded. Unto you

therefore which believe he is precious: but unto them which be disobedient, the stone which the builders disallowed, the same is made the head of the corner, And a stone of stumbling, and a rock of offense, even to them which stumble at the word, being disobedient: whereunto also they were appointed. But ye are a chosen generation, a royal priesthood, a holy nation, a peculiar people; that ye should show forth the praises of him who hath called you out of darkness into his marvelous light: Which in time past were not a people, but are now the people of God: which had not obtained mercy, but now have obtained mercy."
1Peter 2:5-10 KJV

"See that ye refuse not him that speaketh. For if they escaped not who refused him that spake on earth, much more shall not we escape, if we turn away from him that speaketh from heaven: Whose voice then shook the earth: but now he hath promised, saying, Yet once more I shake not the earth only, but also heaven. And this word, Yet once more, signifieth the removing of those things that are shaken, as of

> things that are made, that those things which cannot be shaken may remain. Wherefore we receiving a kingdom which cannot be moved, let us have grace, whereby we may serve God acceptably with reverence and godly fear: For our God is a consuming fire."
>
> Hebrews 12:25-29 KJV

HE IS BUILDING HIS CHURCH

I recently read a history of the early Pentecostal movement in Fiji. An early missionary to the nation reported that the first converts were from Fiji's large Indian population. His observation is interesting and relevant today. Quoting from The Spirit in Paradise:

> "A small congregation evolved among mostly Indians, with healing miracles being the most prominent means of gaining converts...The Indians had religion enough, most being Hindus...So, the Indians did not need to be convinced that they needed to respect a god. They needed to hear the Good News of full and free salvation through Jesus

> Christ, and see the 'signs that follow them that believe'...It is suggested that almost all Indian conversions to Christianity [in Fiji] were the result of an Indian experiencing the supernatural power of God through divine healing, in the name of Jesus Christ, or because someone in the family had such an experience..."

Today, countless plans are on the market for successfully planting and growing churches. They include old paradigms, new paradigms and rehashed paradigms but ultimately only one foundation exists for The Church; a revelatory encounter with Jesus Christ through the work of the Holy Spirit. The growth of the early church cannot be separated from the incredibly effective methodology of preaching the gospel and demonstrating the power. Even in the most hostile environments, the early believers boldly preached the message and did the works while leaving the results to God. Jesus said that He would build His Church. His pattern remains. Preach the Gospel, demonstrate the power.

> "Blessed are you, Simon Bar-Jonah, for flesh and blood has not revealed this to you, but My Father who is in heaven. And I say to you that you are Peter, and on this rock I will build My church , and the gates of Hades

shall not prevail against it."
Matthew 16:18

"And my speech and my reaching were not with persuasive words of human wisdom, but in demonstration of the Spirit and power, that your faith should not be in the wisdom of men but in the power of God." 1 Corinthians 2:4-5

OUT OF THE SHADOWS

"In a parliamentary system, the largest opposition party often refers to itself as a shadow government, and if it is sufficiently large, it may also have a Shadow Cabinet in which top opposition leaders shadow the policies and actions of the corresponding cabinet ministers. They are also prepared to assume the respective ministries of responsibility should their party come to power in an election. For example, in Britain the largest opposition party's defense spokesman might refer to themselves as the Shadow Defense Secretary."

Wikipedia on "shadow government"

David was anointed by God to take over Saul's position as King of Israel. However, Saul was not ready to relinquish his power and became David's enemy. David, for all practical purposes, went into exile. There God drew men to him who would become his army. They are first described as those who where discouraged, discontent and in debt. Some army. But out of this army came what is later referred to as "the mighty men of valor" (1&2 Samuel).

By following God's anointed servant and aligning themselves with His purpose for their nation, this ragtag army became, in effect, a "shadow government," fighting battles, acquiring cities, waiting for their turn. When the time came, they moved into place.

I believe that there is a "shadow Church" being held in waiting for the God's timing. The empty religious institutions and hollow programs of the "recognized" Church will soon give way to those who are being prepared. The Anointed One and His anointed ones are about to step into the light of revealed glory for all to watch in wonder and amazement as the Body of Christ takes its place of destiny.

The exciting thing is that we don't have to wait for the full release of this shadow Church to experience and participate in its blessing. We function as His people now, because WE ARE HIS PEOPLE!! We are the anointed, chosen, called—those who are "led by the Spirit of God are the Sons of God" (Rom. 8:14).

UNSHAKEN

> "But you are a chosen generation, a royal priesthood, a holy nation, His own special people, that you may proclaim the praises of Him who called you out of darkness into His marvelous light"
>
> 1 Peter 2:9 KJV

One night we were between stops at Highway Christian Centre in Bordertown, South Australia, and Park Ridge Baptist Church in Brisbane. I considered how similar these two fellowships are. Both are pastored by relatively young men who came up through the ranks of their local congregations. Both are open to the move of God and are eagerly seeking the revelation of His glory. Both are sending teams to the uttermost parts of the world to preach the gospel of Jesus Christ and release the miracle working power of the Holy Spirit. Worship is a passion in both groups.

For every public failure and humiliating scandal exposed on the international scene, I encounter scores of simple men and women going about doing the works of Jesus and bringing glory to the Father. I am not ashamed of the gospel or the men and women that He has called to spread it. Nor am I ashamed of the power displayed to save the lost, heal the sick and set the captives free.

We are witnessing an unprecedented season of shaking in the earth. Governments, economies and institutions are all feeling the effects of the end time turmoil. God has a people who are not going to be shaken because our trust is in Him and Him alone. His people are shining.

In Townsville, Queensland, a while back, a young man went through a powerful deliverance. He was set free of some really gross stuff. He was also healed a serious back problem and deafness in one ear. This newly filled believer had a vision. He saw little fires burning all over Australia that were growing and came into a big fire of revival that engulfed the whole nation and spread to the world.

I can't tell you how many times I have heard that same prophetic imagery over the last fifteen years both in the United States and in other nations. This young man had never read any books that contained these images or heard any sermons like that—he was simply telling what he saw. God continues to speak His plan. He is touching people and making them His people to shine with His glory.

THE MOVE IS ON

> ***groundswell*** (noun) 1. a buildup of opinion or feeling in a large section of the population. 2. a large or extensive swell in the sea.

In the past, many moves of God have been referred to as "outpourings," which is an accurate and entirely biblical description of a fresh release of the Holy Spirit on hungry and receptive people.

But what I am sensing and seeing happening now would be more accurately described as a groundswell. It is rising up from the people. It is the fruit that is coming forth from kingdom seeds that have been sown for years. It is not centered in one place, one ministry or one movement, but it is the fulfillment of the "faceless army of God" word that came so strongly a few years back. It is a youth move of all ages. That's right, a youth move of all ages. It has new life! The life is flowing from the innermost parts of man where God has released His river of living water. This move is being led by those who are drawing from a deep well of experiential Glory and supernatural power.

This move is pervasive. It cuts across ethnic, national, denominational and age barriers. It has an emphasis on personal intimacy with Jesus while aggressively pursuing the demonstrations of His Spirit and power. It is about God revealing His glory in all the earth and changing the hearts and lives of people through personal experiential encounters. Ordinary people of God are traversing the globe, displaying the tangible glory of the Lord in places where few would expect to see His manifest presence.

This move is not coming—it is happening now! Maybe you read the same article in the news recently that I did about the surfer on holiday from Australia who was out on the water when the tsunami hit Western Samoa. He literally rode out the wave on a surfboard! All he felt initially was the "groundswell." It only raised his level in the water, but what was underneath his board was a power of immense destructive force. When it broke on the shore the incredible surge brought widespread devastation. There is an incredible powerful move that is raising the level of The Church in all the earth. It is about to break upon the shores, becoming apparent to all, but for those who are riding this wave it is happening now. The swell that hit the island nations was an evil destructive force, but God is releasing a demonstration of His power that is bringing healing to the nations.

Chapter 4

The Gospel of Glory

> "But even if our gospel is veiled, it is veiled to those who are perishing, whose minds the god of this age has blinded, who do not believe, lest the light of the gospel of the glory of Christ, who is the image of God, should shine on them. For we do not preach ourselves, but Christ Jesus the Lord, and ourselves your bondservants for Jesus' sake. For it is the God who commanded light to shine out of darkness, who has shone in our hearts to give the light of the knowledge of the glory of God in the face of Jesus Christ."
>
> 2 Corinthians 4:3-6

Jesus revealed the glory of the Father in His fullest expression. In Jesus we see the glory of the Father revealed. Paul refers to the message that he preached as the gospel of the glory of Christ. For Paul, as well as the other apostles, there were more than words involved in the preaching of the gospel. They did not consider the gospel fully preached without demonstrations and manifestation of the truth they were declaring. Peter and John put it this way to the council in Jerusalem, "We cannot help but speak the things we have seen and heard."

The gospel of the glory of Christ involves both seeing and hearing. It is an experiential encounter that involves the whole being of a person. Mind, body, soul and spirit are touched and transformation results. To encounter the "light of the knowledge of the glory of God in the face of Jesus Christ" is to have a life-changing experience. Paul knew first hand what this was like. His initial encounter with the presence of God was certainly an unforgettable experience—knocked to the ground, blinded by light, hearing the audible voice of Jesus, healed by the laying on of hands and receiving the impartation of the Holy Spirit.

Peter also referred to this experiential element of the gospel in 2 Peter 1:3, "As His divine power has given to us all things that pertain to life and godliness, through the knowledge of Him who called us by glory and virtue." The normative introduction to the Christian life was to be called by "glory and virtue." The original Greek as well as the old English word *virtue* were used to mean "manifestations of God's miracle working power." The initial experience of encountering Jesus Christ in the New Testament period was seen to be a wonder-filled, face-to-face, heart-to-heart transformational event that set the course for the remainder of the believer's life.

The instruction "as you received Christ Jesus, so walk ye in Him" is very significant in light of the manner in which the early believers received Him. The supernatural miraculous element of their faith introduced at the onset of the relationship was to characterize their daily practice of Christianity. This daily glory-to-glory progression is in stark contrast to what is advocated and experienced in most modern expressions of the Christian faith. If anything, most mainline preaching today in some way discourages or disparages the pursuit of the very thing that the early Church taught was the essential element of the gospel. Where this element is not looked down on, it is often presented as a rare occurrence. To the apostles it was the normal Christian life.

THE GOODNESS OF GOD

COME THOU FOUNT OF EVERY BLESSING

O to grace how great a debtor

Daily I'm constrained to be!

Let Thy goodness, like a fetter,

Bind my wandering heart to Thee.

"...Believe in the Lord your God, and you shall be established; believe His prophets, and you shall prosper."

2 Chronicles 20:20

"If you are willing and obedient, you shall eat the good of the land"
Isaiah 1:19

"Or do you despise the riches of His goodness, forbearance, and long suffering, not knowing that the goodness of God leads you to repentance?"

Romans 2:4

There is a yearning in the heart of man to see the purity of unadulterated goodness. We look for it in the character of leaders, hoping that in our elevation of a man we have at last found the specimen that is good through and through. With inevitable certainty the pedestal cracks, then crumbles, bringing down the demigod exposing and the imperfections hidden by our delusional quest.

Only One is good. Everything He does is good. No grey areas. No almost-but-not-quite areas. No cracks. No hidden behind the scenes corruption. No bait and switch trickery. No ulterior motives. The One is the essence and the expression, truth in labeling, throughly and completely, without mixture good.

In His inimitable justice, mercy has set the ultimate reckoning for personal transgression at an interval that allows the unmerited offer of absolution an opportunity to fully display His matchless goodness. The revelation of that goodness in the person of Jesus Christ gives even the most reprehensible access to His transformational power. The flow of His "goodness in the land of the living" is released in an overwhelming flood. Unable to contain the overflow, the abundance is released on an unsuspecting, undeserving, but thoroughly loved humanity.

I watched an old western movie over the weekend, John Wayne in "Angel and the Badman." Wayne played an outlaw on the run who encounters a Quaker family that nurses him back to health from a bullet wound. The story shows the power of inherent goodness and love to win even the hardest heart. In the end, Wayne's character gives up the life of a gunslinger for the love of the Quaker girl, the embodiment of innocent goodness. There is a line from a cynical doctor who befriends the family and tends to Wayne that caught my attention. The quote that summarized the mission of the Society of Friends (Quakers) stunned me with its simple clarity and profound implications—"Build your house beside the road and be a friend to the world."

God has built His house beside the road of humanity. As we race by in indifferent pursuit of phantom fulfillment, the consequences of our choices bring us to the front door of His house. Depleted of the illusions of adequacy, we encounter a dwelling empty of life-draining evil. In His house are rooms filled with every restoring, sustaining provision that fulfills the yearning of every heart. Jesus is at the door inviting the wounded world to "taste and see that the Lord is good."

THE END GAME

What is our goal? What are we shooting for?

As is the nature of a carnal people, we continue to compartmentalize the attributes of Christ that fit our giftings and preferences into segments we believe will ultimately morph into the fully functioning whole. The fallacy of this approach is seen in the imagery of Paul's first letter to the Corinthians where he compares the Body of Christ to the human body with the gifts represented by various body parts. No matter how many feet you assemble in a room you will merely have a room full of feet, not a functioning body. (This would be a really fun analogy to pursue—pedicures anyone?)

Attempts continue to abound in the hopes of producing Spiritual life by establishing the proper 'biblical' order. Apart from the extremely tricky problem of arriving at what constitutes authentic 'biblical' order, there is the fact that you cannot produce life in a body by properly assembling the skeleton. The 'build it and they will come' approach apparently only works in new-age baseball movies. The pursuit of 'accountability' by imperfect leadership only leads to some form of legalism that puts on display the folly of human behavior rather than revealing the character of Christ. Who are we to be answerable to ultimately? The Grand Apostolic Council of the Universe? I think they (whoever they are) have repeatedly and sufficiently demonstrated their ability to be fallible. Or perhaps we should follow a more conservative approach and identify with a denominational or institutional group of integrity and impeccable credentials—they never miss it.

Ultimately, I believe there is one scenario that yields the results that so many of us yearn for and are giving our life to pursue. My reason for believing in this approach comes from a lifetime of observing the Church and the people who make up His Body. My conviction comes from the pragmatism of having seen what has come nearest to producing the desired results, while readily acknowledging the residual imperfections.

When the Holy Spirit fills the people of God, genuine Church happens. In what we term revival, a dynamic is released in which the gifts begin to function in an ordered chaos that results from genuine, transformational, real-life encounters. An atmosphere of love and faith combine to produce a fellowship that is simultaneously pursing perfection while graciously nurturing the flawed. As the gifts of the Holy Spirit manifest, true New Testament order is established by the evident usefulness of each individual's supernatural enablement. Apostles apostle, prophets prophecy, healers heal, administrators administrate—you get the idea—and they are recognized and released to function because they are obviously doing what needs to be done. I am no longer naive enough to expect utopia. I simply long for a genuine expression of the life, nature and character of Jesus revealed in the earthen vessels of human beings loving one another and producing spiritual fruit.

Critics will immediately point out that what we call revival has not produced very many permanent displays to the effectiveness of this approach. I have a response. My observation has been that very few have adopted a model of ministry leadership in which the presence of God in the midst of the people is pursued as the continuing and permanent goal. While many have begun in the Spirit, most opt to be perfected in some form of the flesh, thereby voiding the possibility of witnessing what happens when the glory of the Lord takes up habitation in His people instead of just a temporary visitation. After a season of refreshing, most simply return to some form of business as usual or pursue one of the endless array of distracting tangents. What if revival is simply the means to restore the experiential manifestation of the life of Christ to His Body that is meant to be the normative baseline for everything else that we do?

The jaded and wounded have all but given up. The arrogant and self absorbed continue in manipulative pursuit of fodder for their machines of advancement. The hungry hope and pray for more. It is my belief that there *is* more and that the end time work of the Holy Spirit is to assemble a people who are consumed with the love of God and the light of Jesus Christ shining for all the earth to witness. It won't be called revival anymore, it will be the normal, restored and reborn Church.

SILENCING THE CRITICS

> "For this is the will of God, that by doing good you may put to silence the ignorance of foolish men."
>
> 1 Peter 2:15

Peter's strategy for countering critics is to overcome evil with good. In context, the above verse is dealing with the issue of being law-abiding citizens of the highest moral standards. While accurate in this context, the modern understanding of "good works" is far more restricted than the New Testament usage.

For example, Jesus said we are to "let our light shine before men, that they may see your good works and glorify your Father in heaven." The average person today would immediately apply these words to acts of charitable giving or deeds performed on behalf of the poor and needy. Without a doubt, the scripture clearly instructs The Church to care for the widows, orphans and needy. However, When Jesus spoke of "good works" there was a greater dimension to His meaning.

In the discourse between Philip and Jesus recorded in John 14:7-14 it is apparent that the validating sign of His divinity is "the works" that He performed. In all the gospel accounts of Jesus' ministry there is not one single mention of what we would call "good works" today, i.e.; feeding the hungry, housing the homeless, clothing the naked, etc. The good works of Jesus were all miraculous in nature. Every recorded good work done by Jesus was a display of His power to be seen as a sign or wonder (if you find an instance that contradicts this assertion, please let me know). They all had a supernatural element. In fact, the one instance when it was suggested by Judas that resources could be better utilized by giving to the poor, Jesus flatly denied the notion by stating the higher priority of His mission ("the poor are always with you").

What Jesus tells Philip next is absolutely incredible:

> "Most assuredly, I say to you, he who believes in Me, the works I do he will do also; and greater works than these will he do, because I go to My Father."
>
> John 14:12

While good citizenship, kind deeds and charitable giving certainly display the heart of God and are effective at winning over critics, what Jesus had in mind for His followers were also displays of His miracle working power to attest to the validity of the message we carry. I observed during the televangelist scandals of the 1980s that many wise ministry leaders adopted a strategy of global relief efforts and giving to the poor as a way to counter the reputation of greed and manipulation that had developed around high profile personalities. However, as is most often the case, many allowed the pendulum to swing entirely to the other extreme. Charitable acts became a replacement for power displays and any emphasis on the supernatural was viewed with suspicion.

In the season of revival that began in the 90's, much enthusiasm for the miraculous was restored. However, with the almost continuous stream of scandal that has followed, there are those who again seek to marginalize miraculous ministry. Rather, they say we should emphasize relationships, discipleship, etc. All are good and necessary, but not at the expense of demonstrations of the Spirit and power. Acts 10:38 describes Jesus' ministry with clarity and brevity:

> "...how God anointed Jesus of Nazareth with the Holy Spirit and with power, who went about doing good and healing all who were oppressed by the devil, for God was with Him."

In the face of criticism, justified or not, our focus is to remain of "doing the works of Jesus." It is the biblical way to silence the critics. I actually have a proposal for any who might be interested. Instead of de-emphasizing the power gifts, let's go for broke (Aussies—give it a go). Let's get more people operational in more gifts and more anointing and release an army of miracle workers. The flaws and dominance of a few flamboyant individuals would be replaced with a Body of believers carrying the miracle working power of Jesus to the nations. What if miracles became the norm in every gathering of believers?

Chapter 5

Signs, Wonders and Miracles

> "Through mighty signs and wonders, by the power of the Spirit of God; so that from Jerusalem, and round about unto Illyricum, I have fully preached the gospel of Christ."
> Romans 15:19

I've received a number of emails recently from charismatic leaders who are warning of the dangers of over emphasis on signs, wonders and miracles. The reason for their warnings is the antics of some who are obviously 'going off the beam' in their pursuit of the supernatural. However, the particular emails I have gotten go beyond warning against excesses and, in several examples, flat out deny certain signs and wonders as even coming from God. I feel I need to offer a corrective word here.

Paul considers the demonstration of the power of the Holy Spirit essential to the presentation of the full gospel message. He is adamant that the true validation of the message is the accompanying miraculous acts.

> "And my speech and my preaching were not with enticing words of man's wisdom, but in demonstrations of the Spirit and of power; That your faith should not stand in the wisdom of men, but in the power of God."
>
> 1 Corinthians 2:4-5

The majority of those of us who pursue signs, wonders and miracles today are not aberrant theologically, deviant sexually or unstable emotionally as the critics would have you believe. Our desire is to simply present to the world Jesus as He really is. There is the necessity of the confirmation of signs, wonders and miracles if we are going to preach New Testament Christianity. "And these signs shall follow them that believe..." Mark 16:17

I believe the antidote for abuses, error and plain old carnality is for those who possess the real thing to stand up and display the authority of the Kingdom with integrity and transparency, all the while acknowledging that God uses imperfect "earthen" vessels to display His power.

> "Now it happened, as we went to prayer, that a certain slave girl

> possessed with a spirit of divination met us, who brought her masters much profit by fortunetelling. This girl followed Paul and us, and cried out, saying, 'these men are the servants of the Most High God, who proclaim to us the way of salvation.' And this she did for many days. But Paul, greatly annoyed, turned and said to the spirit, 'I command you in the name of Jesus Christ to come out of her. And he came out that very hour."
>
> Acts 16:16-18

The strategy for dealing with the demonic substitute is to display the real thing. In this encounter the demoniac spoke the truth, saw the future, and followed the men of God. I wonder how many of the discerning leaders of today would have even noticed this girl was demonic? She met all the requirements of the contemporary charismatic apostolic councils for orthodoxy. Amazingly, it took "many days" before Paul decided to deal with this issue. When he did confront the demonic spirit with the authority of the name of Jesus, victory manifested.

Rather than be excessively cautious to the point of discouraging the miraculous, why not follow Paul's example in dealing with this practitioner of lying signs and false wonders? If someone is lapsing into carnality or even pure demonic empowerment, leaders should stand up in the superior power of Jesus Christ and demonstrate the clear distinction between the authentic and the distracting. Rather than back off, we should pour on the real anointing.

Paul didn't deny the prophetic because the demonized girl saw the future. He didn't stop preaching the way of salvation because she endorsed it. He didn't deny that they were servants of the Most High God because she proclaimed it. He didn't disavow supernatural power because she operated in it. Instead he dealt with the demon, and she was delivered.

There are countless believers all over the globe who are walking every day in kingdom authority and power with integrity, but they don't seem to be the ones who get noticed. Is it possible that the extreme examples of error that we witness are because those that practice the unusual are the ones that get all the attention from "Christian media"? I've noticed that we have a penchant for recognizing the unusual quirks of ministry personalities. I have seen copy cats return from a meeting mimicking the speech or behavior ticks of the minister they are seeking to emulate. I've often wondered why people are copying the behavior that God moves in spite of, not because of. In some camps, volume is seen as the key to anointing, so shouting reigns. In other groups unusual dress or behavior gets the press, so that is what proliferates. What if we began to focus on the genuine miracles and the lives that were changed as a result. Maybe then we'd see an increase in the genuine power of God on display.

I once had a long conversation with a pastor concerning revival in his fellowship. He said that he genuinely desired a move of God, but he was afraid to allow the Holy Spirit freedom in the services because he was afraid in the excitement that often accompanies an outpouring someone "might get in the flesh." My immediate reaction to this statement was to wonder to myself, "You mean there is no one in your congregation 'in the flesh' now?" Do you deprive the Body of Christ from the opportunity of experiencing the genuine revelation of God's glory simply because someone strays into error?

In the past nineteen years I've seen some stuff. In one meeting we conducted, my wife observed a woman drop what looked like a diamond on the floor during worship and then dance away only to return in a few moments to 'discover' the manifestation of a gem stone—the one she had just intentionally dropped. She brought it to me before I knew the whole story, but I immediately noticed that there was glue from the obviously human setting still on the back of this cheap costume stone—it wasn't even a real fake! I handed it back to her and then my wife confronted her. She left and didn't come back. Here is the point: I didn't stop the service. I didn't rebuke those who were having a genuine encounter with Jesus. I didn't spend a moment more distracted by this fruitcake—I kept pursuing with passion the awesome presence and glory of the Lord.

The emails I referred to earlier have specifically mentioned signs and wonders such as gem stones, oil, gold dust, feathers and unusual lights or orbs as being especially grievous transgressions. I want to again go on record and unashamedly testify that I have witnessed all the above (and more) in meetings that I have conducted where Jesus was being glorified, the presence of God was so thick it was difficult or impossible to stand, and, most importantly, lives were changed.

I have to acknowledge that I too have cringed when I have heard reports or seen videos of what's been done in some recent meetings; outlandish behavior simply to draw attention to itself. However, my reaction is not because I haven't seen and experienced for myself genuine Holy Spirit manifestations. I've staggered, fallen and laughed with the best of them. I've even had a couple of glory encounters, like the prophet Ezekiel, that resembled descriptions of hallucinogenic drug trips that some of my friends from the old days have told me about. My concern isn't that strange things are happening, it is that some of the videos I've seen and reports I've heard don't seem to be real. When the Spirit of God moves in power and glory you don't have to make things happen, you don't have to work things up, you don't have to imitate or initiate bizarre behavior. When Jesus gets real, we get real. True emotions explode. Shouts of joy unspeakable, inebriation on the new wine, dancing, shaking, crying, jumping, falling; all of this happens out of the flow of a genuine encounter with an overwhelming reality—Jesus!

In my travels to the Solomon Islands I heard about the phenomena of 'cargo cults.' In case you haven't heard of these groups, they are primitive tribes or villages that encountered American troops for the first time during WWII and thought they were gods to be worshiped because of the powerful weapons and amazing technology they brought with them. Here is an explanation from ***Wikipedia***:

> Famous examples of cargo cult activity include the setting up of mock airstrips, airports, offices, and dining rooms, as well as the fetishization and attempted construction of Western goods, such as radios made of coconuts and straw. Believers may stage "drills" and "marches" with sticks for rifles and use military-style insignia and national insignia painted on their bodies to make them look like soldiers, thereby treating the activities of Western military personnel as rituals to be performed for the purpose of attracting the cargo. The cult members built these items and "facilities" in the belief that the structures would attract cargo intended to be sent to them.

Spiritually, I am concerned that some, like the cargo cults of the South Pacific, may be attempting to mimic the manifestations that often accompany a genuine outpouring of the glory of God in hopes of experiencing the real thing (or, in some cases, to reap the benefits of appearing to have the real thing). Rather than write off the real thing, let's recognize what's actually happening. Receiving the genuine is an antidote to the imitation.

REALITY CHECK

Sometimes I wonder if we are really getting across the right message? I'm talking about those of us who believe in life in the Spirit and the reality of the manifest presence of Jesus. I think some people mistakenly hear our entreaties to be filled as calls to become more expressive, more excited, more demonstrative in the church service setting. I don't think we are miscommunicating as much are we being misheard. Regardless, let's clear the air.

What I am after *is that every believer in Jesus Christ experience the reality of the presence of God through the empowering work of the Holy Spirit.* There is a level of reality that results in transformation when encountered. This transformational encounter touches us at such a deep level that every area—mind, body and soul—is affected. The mind is changed, emotions are released and even the physical body reacts to the manifest presence of God.

Religious people will often say, "I just don't act that way" or "We just don't respond demonstratively." Hogwash. People get vocal and loud about what is real and important to them. I hate to use the cliche, but watch them at a sporting event and then watch them at church. Or how about the laughter that rolls at a private gathering of friends compared to the sedated atmosphere in many churches?

Again, I'm not pushing for artificial and contrived displays. I am suggesting that what most are settling for is artificial—worship devoid of meaning, work with no power and a rigid formalism that is only put on in a religious setting. What I am saying is that the mask needs to come off. Let's get real about our relationship to God. Let's get real and let Him get real. When God reveals himself something happens. When we allow that revelation to have its full impact, an honest heartfelt response is the natural result. How does this sound: A passionate people pursuing a passionate lover who also is pursuing them. A people in love; mind, body, heart and soul."

HIS GLORY

> "I do not pray for these alone (the twelve), but also for those who will believe in Me through their word; that they all may be one, as You, Father, are in Me, and I in You; that they also may be one in Us, that the world may believe that You sent Me. And the glory which You gave me I have given them, that they may be

one just as We are one."
John 17:20-22

That statement is amazing all by itself, even without the rest of the passage: 'the glory which You gave me I have given them.' From Jesus' perspective, the defining characteristic of His followers is the presence of the glory of the Father residing in the believer.

There is an innate, insatiable hunger yearning in the heart of every true child of God that produces the cry for more! Something is missing. Something is off. Something is not quite right. So we attempt to fix it by dealing with the symptoms of the problem. No unity, simply fix it—get unified. No holiness, that's easy, stop sinning. No power, easily resolved—well—maybe not so easily. What we lack is His glory that produces the evidences that are so glaringly absent in most expressions of Christianity today.

In the modern era, this deficiency is evident from the beginning of our understanding of how God works in our lives. The early Church had no misunderstanding. They knew that they were followers of Christ because His Holy Spirit came on them in a supernatural outpouring that produced transformation. Change came because Jesus changed them by the revelation of His glory (see Paul's encounter on the road to Damascus as the most vivid example). From the inception of the relationship, the early believers were confronted with the manifested glory of the

Father through the work of the Holy Spirit which produced life changing results.

> "Grace and peace be multiplied to you in the knowledge of God and of Jesus our Lord, as His divine power has given to us all things that pertain to life and godliness, through the knowledge of Him who called us by glory and virtue"   2 Peter 1:2-3

Leaders trained in traditional institutional church, heard an often repeated criticism of mass evangelism (big crusades) that they seldom resulted in a significant number of converts becoming church members. So myriads of programs emerged to change the methodology of evangelism by moving to a 'discipleship' model. Through intense Bible study, close oversight and behavior modification techniques, well meaning leaders sought to bring about change through increased diligence. The problem, however, was not in the techniques of evangelism, but in the very nature of the way we view conversion. For generations, traditional religion has used the educational model as their approach to making new converts. This approach has produced millions of "converts" who mentally ascend to the truth of the gospel message but have never experienced the transformation that occurs when one is "born from above."

I remember vividly the first "soul winning" school I attended. It was in the early 1970s and the denomination I belonged to was promoting a brand new door-to-door witnessing program. In the training we were given a three-ring binder with a copy of the soul winning manual that was so new it was still being edited. We were the guinea pigs in an innovative program that would revolutionize the Church, or at least that's what the man leading the seminar said. In his presentation he made several memorable statements. One I'll never forget was his inside information on how the training material was developed. He excitedly pointed out that the authors had simply taken an insurance sales manual and everywhere it talked about the product they had changed the wording to refer to Jesus. As he continued on in this vein, he pointed to statistics from insurance industry research that showed that you could mathematically predict how many people would "say yes" and buy your product when given a proper presentation of the material. To increase the number of sales, you simply had to knock on more doors and talk to more people. As we later tested this approach in the field, unfortunately his statistical projections were frighteningly correct. X number of presentations produced Y number of "yes" responses. The reason I say unfortunately is that we were supposedly presenting the gospel of Jesus Christ and the people responding to our presentation were, according to those keeping meticulous records, converted.

How foreign this approach would be to Peter or Paul or Philip. Here is the biblical description of their approach:

> "And I, brethren, when I came to you, did not come with excellence of speech or of wisdom declaring to you the testimony of God. For I determined not to know anything among you except Jesus Christ and Him crucified. I was with you in weakness, in fear, and in much trembling. And my speech and my preaching were not with persuasive words of human wisdom, but in demonstration of the Spirit and of power, that your faith should not be in the wisdom of men but in the power of God."
>
> I Corinthians 2:1-5

DEAD FROG THEOLOGY

There is always the pull to take an experiential reality and reduce it to a system of doctrines and teachings. In so doing, the vitality of the reality is robbed. I have a story I like to repeat. When I was in Junior High School I had a very conscientious science teacher, Mr. David Woods. His goal was to make our understanding of biology as real and complete as possible. Like many students of our era, we were given the task of dissecting a frog. Mr. Woods would not be satisfied with a simple dissection of a dead frog. Our subject had to be alive so that we could see all the organs functioning. So the frogs were put to sleep with ether, and we began the task of opening them up to observe the beating heart, the pumping blood, etc. When we completed the work, we had a very vivid understanding of the inner workings of a frog. There was only one problem; the frog was dead. In the spiritual realm there is a direct correlation. By the time a move of God is analyzed, categorized, and systematized—while there may be a thorough understanding of what happened and why—the frog is dead. All the life is robbed of the event by the application of the wisdom of men.

During the outpouring in Nauru that we have been blessed to be part of, I was approached by a very sincere man who wanted to discuss theology with me. Actually, he wanted to prove that the age of miracles, signs and wonders had ceased with the death of the original twelve apostles and the coming of the Bible. The only problem with his argument was that we were seeing miracles and signs happening in the very meeting he was attending. While his reason for attending the meetings was to gather ammunition for his arguments he was confronted with the reality of people being touched by the Holy Spirit, many overpowered by the experience and on the floor under the anointing. While their lives were being changed, his heart was hardening as he went through his mental file folder of reasons that what he was seeing and hearing wasn't real, wasn't for today and wasn't "biblical." He remained untouched by God, trapped in analysis mode.

For the hungry, there is the wonderful reality of a personal, life changing, transformational encounter with the glory of God revealed by the Holy Spirit in the face of Jesus Christ. Words just don't quite have the required adequacy to convey what happens when the Holy Spirit turns on the revelatory light and you are never the same again.

THE WORK OF AN EVANGELIST

> "Be watchful in all things, endure afflictions, do the work of an evangelist, fulfill your ministry."
>
> 2 Timothy 4:5

Methodology and technique are not the biblical emphasis in doing the work of an evangelist. Or maybe I should say, current methodology and techniques don't seem to follow the New Testament pattern. In fact, the methodology for how the early Church spread the gospel of the Kingdom is radically different from the approach employed by most of the Church today.

The most obvious difference is that the early Church seemed to understand the command to "go." They didn't wait for the multitudes to come to them, they went because they were sent. The apostles took an aggressive approach to the task. Philip, the first recorded evangelist, took the initiative and moved into what should have been hostile territory, Samaria. The result was an outpouring of the Holy Spirit that brought rejoicing to the whole region.

The sharpest contrast between the early believer's approach and many today is that they not only went with a message, they went with power. Paul clearly said to the Corinthians that the demonstration of the power of the Holy Spirit that they experienced personally was to the be foundation of their faith.

> "...but in the demonstration of the
> Spirit and of power, that your faith
> should not be in the wisdom of men
> but in the power of God."
>
> 1 Corinthians. 2:1-5

A growing army of believers is in the earth today who recognize that the "insurance sales" model of evangelism is ineffective. It produces "converts" with a head knowledge or an emotional touch, but no true transformation. In fact, I believe that the concern that many have for a lack of true "discipleship" is misplaced. I don't believe it is a lack of formal discipleship programs that account for the lack of maturity and growth in the Church. I believe the real problem is that many converts are brought into church life without any personal encounter with the Holy Spirit. That encounter is where the hunger is imparted that compels the new believer to pursue Jesus with all their heart, with all their soul and with all their mind.

I received a greeting from my good friend who pastors a church in Adelaide, South Australia. He shared with me that their church continues to see signs and wonders, specifically the appearance of the "glory dust" as a tool for evangelism. They sets up a tent at the annual New Age fair in the community and asks God to send the sign of the glory dust on unbelievers. When the tangible manifestation of the glory of God appears the result is often an instant openness to hear and receive the Gospel message.

A while back, I was in Virginia with a friend whose ministry includes both an established church as well as his personal outreach to the blues community as a singer/songwriter/guitarist. On Saturday night we were in a trendy downtown deli that features live music. Landon and his band performed two awesome sets of first rate blues. Then for the last set he transitioned into several songs that overtly carried the gospel message. As the anointing of the Holy Spirit fell on the place people were visibly moved. My friend and his daughters filled the room with the message of Jesus Christ. The sound went out the open windows to the street below where a large vintage car rally was being held. As they finished each song, the applause grew louder with shouts and raised hands in affirmation, not from Church people, but from the folks who just came in for the music, a beer and deli sandwich!

The work of an evangelist is a Holy Ghost enterprise from start to finish. His anointing validates the message we bring. The Spirit draws men to Christ. As they are born of the Spirit, the transformational power of God is released that starts the new believer on the journey to maturity and fruitfulness and continues until the work is completed.

We are in the midst of a global harvest move of God. God is pouring out signs, wonders and miracles. Those who go in power are seeing results. Some touch one or two, some hundreds and some thousands. Without exception, those who are carrying this vision are going, and they are going in power. Not every encounter produces what we call a miracle, but the new birth, the greatest miracle, is the result of the anointed people of God proclaiming the gospel with boldness.

GO MODE

There is a forward momentum in the ethos of the new covenant that cannot be ignored or minimized. Jesus, of course, set the standard, "Go into all the earth..." Paul especially embodied this spirit of "go."

> "Not that I have already attained, or am already perfected; but I press on, that I may lay hold of that for which Christ Jesus has also laid hold of me. Brethren, I do not count myself to have apprehended; but one thing I do, forgetting those things which are behind and reaching forward to those things which are ahead. I press

> toward the goal for the prize of the
> upward call of God in Christ Jesus."
> Philippians 3:12-14

The "go mode" was both an internal spiritual motivation to maturity and Christlikeness as well as an outward expression of obedience to complete the prophetic destiny of The Church. Three notable themes run throughout the epistles of Paul: focus, perseverance and boldness.

In the letter to the Philippians, Paul puts his personal philosophy in context of a race. It is amazing that he considers himself to have "not apprehended." This is not a denial of the finished work of the cross or the reality of the new man that he clearly states in other writings. Rather, it is a simple recognition that in his own life there is still "more." But then he gets to the heart of the issue for all of us, "but <u>one thing</u> I do." Paul states the necessity of narrowing the focus in order to attain the promise of the things that are still ahead. What is the "one thing?" Paul said it is forgetting the past [good and bad] and reaching or pressing forward to the goal. To keep going requires focus. This is who I am, this is where I am headed, this is my purpose.

> "And we desire that each one of you
> show the same diligence to the full
> assurance of hope until the end, that
> you do not become sluggish, but
> imitate those who through faith and

> patience [perseverance] inherit the promises." Hebrews 6:11-12

Perseverance, i.e., steadfast patience, is put on equal footing with faith. In the 20th Century there was a tremendous movement called by many "The Faith Movement," that continues to impact millions of believers worldwide. However, I have never heard of anyone advocating a "Patience Movement." But in terms of "apprehending all that we have been apprehended for," perseverance is seen as equally necessary. A common misunderstanding is that patience is inactive, passive "waiting." Unfortunately, this is not merely inaccurate, it is the opposite of the truth. For some, patience means sitting passively and seeing how many body blows can be endured before complete defeat. That's why I like to use the word "perseverance" interchangeably. The reality is that biblical concept of ***perseverance*** is defined as:

> 1) steadfastness in doing something in spite of difficulty or delay on achieving success;
>
> 2) theological: continuance in a state of grace leading finally to a state of glory.

Twice Paul requests that prayer be made for him that he might "speak boldly as he ought to speak." A major insight into the "go mode" is found in 1 Timothy 1:6-7:

> "Therefore I remind you to stir up the gift of God which is in you through the laying on of my hands. For God has not given us a spirit of fear [timidity, shrinking back], but of power and of love and of a sound mind."

The contrast is clear. The Spirit of God leads to a bold proclamation and demonstration while the spirit of timidity leads one to draw back and not attain the promise of the fulness. Through intimidation the enemy seeks to shut the believer up and shut him down. The doodle-bug, turtle defense mode employed by many in the face of opposition and pressure will not lead to victory and completion. There is an immediate and tangible benefit to "go":

> "Now thanks be to God who always leads us in triumph in Christ, and through us diffuses the fragrance of His knowledge in every place."
> 2 Corinthians 2:14

AT LAST

Belief in the ultimate revelation of God's glory at the visible and literal return of Jesus Christ does not, nor should not, diminish the expectations for an ever increasing revelatory flow of His glory now. To say that He is coming again does not mean that He is currently absent. Christ in us (now) is the hope of glory (present and future). The prophetic teachings that see the Church being purified and glorified in preparation for His return need not imply that the Kingdom will be ushered in apart from His physical appearing and the catching away of the saints so clearly taught in the New Testament. Just as the doctrine of increasing evil has unquestionable biblical foundations, so does the revelation of increased glory resident in the end-time Church.

Spiritualization of literal scriptural teachings on end-time events can only lead to the same methodology being applied to other foundational truths, robbing them of their tangible fulfillment. Efforts to rectify the errors of dispensational teachers have led many to abandon the belief in the *"parousia"* (appearing of Christ, catching away of saints). While I personally believe that the term "rapture" and its accompanying theology is unfounded in scripture, I do believe in the visible return of Jesus and the catching away of the saints, both living and dead, to meet Him in the air. It is the only possible literal interpretation of the words spoken by Jesus concerning the event.

This is not an "escape" clause that denies the reality of tribulation and suffering in the current world situation. I am not advocating the view of dispensationalism that we will get snatched away before things get "really bad." Things are really bad now and getting worse. What I am saying is that the return of Jesus is the ultimate hope for peace, reconciliation, a new heaven and a new earth. An earth unpolluted, unspoiled, pure, delightful and just, with no hint or stain of evil or suffering—that is the reality that will be ushered in by the ultimate revelation of His glory.

The preparation required for His coming is explained in the parable of the ten virgins. Our lamps are to be filled with oil, which is an analogy for being continuously filled with the Holy Spirit. We are not to hoard supplies for the coming calamities, nor feverishly fret about the Antichrist, nor give dire pronouncements concerning specific disasters being directly tied to this or that judgment of God upon the sins of the nation involved. Rather, we are to be filled with the Spirit, proclaiming His Kingdom until He comes. We are to overcome evil with good, preach the good news, and demonstrate the goodness that leads men to true repentance and to faith in Jesus Christ, the soon coming King. This is a healthy approach to an increasingly dysfunctional world system and calamitous natural disasters that will increase as the "birth pangs" grow in frequency and intensity. Jesus is coming again. Jesus is coming soon. **Maranatha**.

WHEN THE GLORY COMES

> "When all the children of Israel saw how the fire came down, and the glory of the Lord on the temple, they bowed their faces to the ground on the pavement, and worshiped and praised the Lord, saying: 'For He is

good, for His mercy endures forever."

2 Chronicles 7:3

On the day of dedication of the newly completed temple built by King Solomon, the response of the people of God to the amazing revelation of His glory was to prostrate themselves in His presence and begin a chorus of praise that still echos today, "For He is good, For His mercy endures forever." When His glory was revealed, the recognition that came to the people was the overwhelming mercy and goodness of God. 2 Chronicles 7:10 says, "...he sent the people away to their tents, joyful and glad of heart for the good that the Lord had done for David, for Solomon, and for His people of Israel." There was an immediate ecstatic response to the tangible expression of glory. The people were joyful that a real-world, real-time blessing had come upon them. The visible observable glory of God brings to the forefront of consciousness just how amazing it is that we are allowed to interact with the Creator/Sustainer of the universe.

God reveals His glory in many ways. His multifaceted, multidimensional, manifold nature, character and power is revealed sovereignly. He chooses the time and manner in which He reveals himself. However, it is significant that on the day of the dedication of Solomon's temple His glory was revealed in a tangible and dramatic way in response to Solomon's prayer at the completion of the building project. A divine interaction with destiny encompasses both His will and our response. Obedience and disobedience affect outcomes without violating the sovereignty of the Father. He foreknows and He predestines, but He also acts based on our response to His revelation.

I had a conversation several years ago with a pastor concerning the issue of sovereignty as it related to revival. The pastor's position was that revival was poured out sovereignly without regard to the people of God. While I agreed with the absolute sovereignty of the Father, I couldn't escape the conclusion that what was really being offered was an excuse for not receiving what the Holy Spirit was already pouring out. As I went away from the conversation I asked the Father for understanding. Specifically I prayed, "What is it Lord? Do we pray, press in and receive what you are offering or do you just do it without our involvement?" Immediately word pictures began to form in my head. I heard the Lord say, "When you were a baby your father sovereignly went to work and earned money which he sovereignly gave your mother who sovereignly went to the store and bought milk and sovereignly put it in the refrigerator so that when you cried out in hunger in the night, she sovereignly got up and fed you."

Solomon obeyed the prophetic revelation that he would build the temple that was in David's heart. He prayed and sought the Lord when the project was completed, and God's response was to pour out His glory in an awesome display of power and might. The people were overwhelmed with joy at the goodness and mercy of God. The Bible says that the glory of the Father is revealed in the face of Jesus Christ. When we seek Him, we find. He sovereignly preordained our need and His response to our hunger. The interaction that happens as this divine mystery unfolds is transformational. We are lifted out of the limitations of our human existence and confronted with the reality of His unlimited glory.

THE WOW FACTOR

> "For My thoughts are not your thoughts, Nor are your ways My ways," says the Lord. "For as the heavens are higher than the earth, So are My ways higher than your ways, And My thoughts than your thoughts."
>
> Isaiah 55:8-9

I read a news report about an unexplained event known as the "Wow" signal. Thirty five years ago, the Big Ear observatory at Ohio State University picked up a 72-second burst of radio transmission coming from the direction of the constellation Sagittarius. To quote the article, "At its peak, the transmission was 30 times more powerful than ambient radiation from deep space, prompting the volunteer astronomer Jerry Ehman to scrawl "Wow!" next to the data on a computer printout, giving the signal its name." Although never identified or heard from again, some believe it to be proof of extraterrestrial life.

Whatever the truth about this signal, it causes me to think about how much more of a "wow factor" there is in a revelatory encounter with the glory of God. If scientists get that excited about a 72-second unexplained radio signal, how much more should we be excited about a face-to-face encounter with the glory of God by the work of the Holy Spirit when Jesus is revealed to us personally? An encounter with the reality of Jesus Christ is clear and unmistakable. It is also life changing and transformational. It never fades or goes away. It grows stronger with continued exposure. In the kingdom, we are not just given cold hard facts written on dead paper. We are given living words from the living God that releases life in us. In the kingdom we are called to encounter the Truth, experience transformation and become the embodiment of the reality revealed.

Walking in kingdom reality means working with kingdom understanding. The fundamental difference between functioning from a humanist worldview and a kingdom paradigm is the origin of truth. While we may agree on many issues and practicalities, a vital inescapable difference in this foundational issue ultimately is the guide in formulating every closely held conviction. Jesus taught that in order to see from a kingdom perspective one had to experience a spiritual birth. He later said that the Holy Spirit would lead us into truth. He illustrated with Peter that revelation was the foundation of kingdom authority. The apostle Paul makes it clear that the gospel he preached came from a direct revelatory encounter.

Both the thoughts and actions of God are on a higher plane than even the most brilliant among us. His desire, through the revelatory work of the Holy Spirit, is to empower even the simplest among us to operate from His realm rather than the limits we are bound with as humans. He imparts wisdom and knowledge by revelation rather than the reasoning of men. This is not to say, as some suggest, that we don't use our brains. God has designed us so that the brain becomes the processor of revelation. Rather than bypassing our mind, He elevates us to His level.

PREEMINENCE

preeminence - having paramount rank, dignity, or importance; outstanding, supreme.

Merriam -Webster

"For this reason we also, since the day we heard it, do not cease to pray for you, and to ask that you may be filled with the knowledge of His will in all wisdom and spiritual understanding; that you may walk worthy of the Lord, fully pleasing Him, being fruitful in every good work and increasing in the knowledge of God; strengthened with all might, according to His glorious power, for all patience and long suffering with joy; giving thanks to the Father who has qualified us to be partakers of the inheritance of the saints in the light. He has delivered us from the power of darkness and conveyed us into the kingdom of the Son of His love, in whom we have redemption through His blood, the forgiveness of sins.

He is the image of the invisible God, the firstborn over all creation. For by Him all things were created that are in heaven and that are on earth, visible and invisible, whether thrones or dominions or principalities or powers. All things were created through Him and for Him. And He is before all things, and in Him all things consist. And He is the head of the body, the Church, who is the beginning, the firstborn from the dead, that in all things He may have preeminence.

For it pleased the Father that in Him all the fullness should dwell, and by Him reconcile all things to Himself, by Him whether things on earth or things in heaven, having made peace through the blood of His cross.

> And you, who once were alienated and enemies in your mind by wicked works, yet now He has reconciled in the body of His flesh through death, to present you holy, and blameless and above reproach in His sight."
> Colossians 1:9-22

When traveling by air, cloud cover commonly is found up to a certain altitude. Once the plane has broken through the cloud cover a whole new world seems to appear—blue sky, sunlight and a vista to the horizon. To be "conveyed" into "the kingdom of the Son of His love" is that same kind of experience in the spiritual realm. As believers in Jesus Christ and inheritors of the New Covenant, we are called to live in that realm. He has qualified us, He has delivered us and He has, by His own blood, forgiven us. We are now clear to soar in that realm with Him.

We have been connected to the One who created heaven and earth as the writer of Hebrews says, "By the word of His power." That "word of His power," **"*rehema / dunamis*"** in Greek, is now working in us to create and release in the earth the preeminence of Christ. This is no trivial matter. This is really "what it's ALL about!"

Religion has left many living in a miniature world of make believe—like a toy train set and all the fake scenery used to make it appear as close as possible to real while still being what it is, a miniaturized copy. Countless Christians are seeing the miniature imitation as their reality. For these enthusiasts, religion seems to have become a hobby, moving pieces around on a fake landscape hoping to approximate the actual. Taking their direction from memories of the past, photographs and instructions from "experts," their fulfillment is in replicating their perception of perfection in a controlled environment.

Surely the Christian experience is about more than simply perfecting a one-hour meeting. The pursuit of truth is more than having the right position in all of our doctrine, teaching and theology. The objective of our faith has to be more than just getting a shiny new car or our dream house. And ultimately, history is about more than a piece or real estate in the Mideast.

We have been infused with the life force of the creator of the universe. We are now walking daily in communion with the one who holds all things together. We are living, moving and breathing in a realm above all earthly kingdoms. Our purpose, the purpose of The Church, the purpose of all nations, governments and spiritual authorities in the heavenlies, the purpose of all creation is the preeminence of Christ. We have been called into intimate relationship with Jesus. We have been called into fruitful ministry in His Kingdom. We have been set on the stage of eternal significance. All of this so the Son of God can be revealed as all in all.

Chapter 6
Activating The Power

One of my earliest and most embarrassing memories is when I spent an entire recess period in third grade attempting to fly like Superman using my coat as a cape. I looked up from my quest to see that I was alone on the playground, all the other kids had gone back to class while I was obliviously immersed in a far higher pursuit. I don't remember the excuse I gave the teacher for returning late, but I do vividly remember the embarrassment of being late and the equally devastating disappointment of failing at my attempt to fly.

I believe that innate in every human being is the awareness that we were created for more than what is considered normal by culture. The whole super hero phenomenon derives from a deep rooted awareness that there is an unseen mysterious dimension that elevates mere mortals to super human, supernatural status.

"God, who at sundry times and in divers manners spake in time past unto the fathers by the prophets, Hath in these last days spoken unto us by his Son, whom he hath appointed heir of all things, by whom also he made the worlds; Who being the brightness of his glory, and the express image of his person, and upholding all things by the word of His power, when he had by himself purged our sins, sat down on the right hand of the Majesty on high;" Hebrews 1:1-3

word- *rhema*; an utterance;

power-*dunamis*; force; specially, miraculous power (usually by implication, a miracle itself) [In contrast with *"exousia"* which refers to authority. The difference between a judge and electricity.]

The Word of God and the power of God are inextricably intertwined. To be connected to the power of God is to be hooked up to the source all of creation. The force, the energy, the dynamic that set everything into motion and holds it together is the Word of His power. Clarke's Commentary: "This is an astonishing description of the infinitely energetic and all pervading power of God. He spake, and all things were created; he speaks, and all things are sustained."

In Hebrews the direct connection is made between God's revelatory work and His miracle working power. The Word of God carries with it a force that creates what has been spoken. In the revelatory flow is the creative flow. The moment of epiphany carries with it the power to create the reality that has been revealed. The almost incomprehensible promise of scripture is that those who are followers of Jesus Christ are imbued with that same power. The same power that spoke the worlds into existence, the same power that actively upholds all of creation, the same power that raised Jesus Christ from the dead is now at work in the true believer. The implications are astonishing.

One of the unfortunate traps that many Christians fall into is believing that somehow or another a technique or a procedure must be followed that produces the ability to work miracles. That technique, just that right word or those combination of phrases or that particular plan must be followed to see that reality ignited. The truth is there is not a technique you can learn. Seeing the miraculous released in your life doesn't come by a new technique. It doesn't come by a new procedure. It doesn't come by a new plan that you have implemented. It comes out of the flow of a relationship. That relationship is established with Jesus Christ, receiving the fullness of His Holy Spirit and hungering and thirsting after His glory.

If there is one thing I could say that above everything else is a key and a significant factor in seeing the miraculous released in your life, it's your words—the words that come out of your mouth. I can't give you a technique, I can't give you a procedure, but I can tell you this—God will confirm His word with signs and wonders following. If you speak His word, if it is His word coming out of your mouth, He has committed himself to back up His word with all the power, all the resources of Heaven. As long as you are saying your stuff, He has not made that commitment. Some people wonder why they try their best but God doesn't show up. He is not committed to your plan. He is only committed to His plan. He's not committed to your words. He's committed to His word. So if we, His people, are hearing His voice and saying what we hear, then we can have the expectation that He's going to do what He said He would do. However, if we are saying what is coming out of our own understanding and our own minds and our own desires and wishes, He's not obligated to make that happen.

The most abrupt lesson in my personal prayer life was after I had been praying for several hours one day using a prayer manual as a guide. I was praying diligently following the check list given in the book. My prayers seemed to be hitting the ceiling and bouncing back. The more I prayed and the more intense I got in a particular area, the less I felt His presence. Out of desperation, I finally got honest with God and I said, "God I'm just not feeling anything. It seems as though you are not listening at all. Why won't you answer me?" I will never forget the response the Holy Spirit spoke in my heart. He said, "I'm just not interested in the subject you are talking about. If you will change the subject I will be happy to talk with you."

Our agenda and our priorities are not always the same as His. Your crisis is not necessarily God's crisis. A friend of mine puts it this way: Your lack of planning does not constitute a crisis on my part. Our lack of understanding, our lack of revelation, doesn't produce a crisis in Heaven. The crisis is in us and what we need to understand is that there is no crisis in Heaven. His word is settled for eternity and if we get one word from Him, our crisis disappears. The revelatory gifts of the Holy Spirit all flow out of the personal intimate relationship we maintain with Jesus. As we seek His face, hear His voice and follow His word, He walks with us and backs up everything we do and say with His validating miracle working power.

THE SPIRIT AND THE WORD

"The grass withers, and the flower fades, but the word of our God will stand forever." Isaiah 40:8

"God who at various times and in various ways spoke in time past to the fathers by the prophets, has in these last days spoken to us by His Son, whom He has appointed heir of all things, through whom also He made the worlds; who being the brightness of His glory and the

express image of His person, and upholding gall things by the word of His power, when He had by Himself purged our sins, sat down at the right hand of the Majesty on high."
Hebrews 1:1-3

"However, when He, the Spirit of truth, has come, He will guide you into all truth; for He will not speak on His own authority, but whatever He hears He will speak; and He will tell you things to come. He will glorify Me, for He will take of what is Mine and declare it to you. All things that the Father has are Mine. Therefore I said that He will take of Mine and declare it to you."

John 16:13-15

"And that from a child thou hast known the holy scriptures, which are able to make thee wise unto salvation through faith which is in Christ Jesus. All scripture is given by inspiration of God, and is profitable for doctrine, for reproof, for correction, for instruction in righteousness: That the man of God may be perfect, throughly furnished unto all good works."

2 Timothy 3:15-17

The Word or The Spirit? I've heard a lot of chatter recently concerning authority in the life of a believer. Is the Bible our ultimate guide or is the Holy Spirit? Why does it have to be either/or? To loose from the moorings of scripture is to be set adrift into the turbulent waters of ambiguity and fickle subjectivism. To chain yourself to traditions of men based on inadequate understanding of biblical revelation creates a modern day Pharisee. Either extreme is to be avoided.

The Spirit leads us into all truth. To pit the scripture against the Spirit is making a distinction between the spoken Word of God, the incarnate Word of God and the written Word of God concerning authority. There are no grounds for such a distinction to be made. In the eyes of some, apparently, the distinction is necessary in order to deal with troublesome passages. What is particularly disturbing is when this paradigm is used to explain away direct biblical directives and declarations simply because they inconveniently weaken some particular contemporary teaching.

Interpretation and application can vary to amazing degrees without abandoning a high view of the inspiration and authority of scripture. The Holy Spirit does indeed lead to new and fresh understanding of the written Word.

Jesus was himself the most radical re-interpreter of the Law and The Prophets of His day. The Apostle Paul's theology of the Law and grace was so different that even Peter had difficulty understanding his arguments—but Peter still viewed them as scripture as he stated in 2 Peter 3:16-17:

> "...just as our beloved brother Paul also wrote to you according to the wisdom given him, as he does in all his letters when he speaks in them of these matters. There are some things in them that are hard to understand, which the ignorant and unstable twist to their own destruction, as they do the other scriptures."

The authority of scripture never brought the conflict between Jesus and the Pharisees. Their own misinterpretations and ignorance of the meaning behind the written Word of God were in conflict. Numerous examples of this exist. One is found in Mark 12:24:

> "Is this not the reason you are wrong, because you know neither the scriptures nor the power of God?"

Classic liberal theology has been the dominate influence in the mainstream denominational church for generations. It is rooted in the rationalistic/scientific paradigm that denies the existence of the miraculous. In this system of thought, because miracles are against science and reason, scripture, which is full of the miraculous, must be rejected as authoritative and accurate in a historical sense. As an extension of this mindset, when the Bible speaks on social and moral issues it must be interpreted in the light of modern scholastic mores. Ultimately, the authority of Scripture is subjugated to the wisdom of men. Due to the necessity of self-preservation, liberal theologians cling to scripture as a subject of study while rejecting its ultimate authority as God's Word.

What we are facing in the emerging church movement, the charismatic movement and even some factions of current evangelical thought differs from classic liberal theology. Portions of Scripture are being dismissed because of doctrinal views based on other portions. I have witnessed this as it relates to several teaching emphases. Again, it is possible to have widely divergent interpretations and applications of specific scriptural passages without calling into question the validity of seemingly contradictory portions of the Bible.

This issue relates, not indirectly, to the 'experience' Vs 'reason' issue that is often in the background of much disharmony in the body of Christ. From my perspective it is essential in understanding and applying scripture that we be illuminated by the Holy Spirit. Peter, to illustrate my point, heard every word that Jesus spoke. He saw every miracle that Jesus preformed. He walked and talked with Jesus every day, but He didn't 'get it' until the outpouring of the Holy Spirit on the day of Pentecost. Then, and only then, was he able to boldly and authoritatively say, "This is THAT which was spoke by the prophet Joel..." The written Word came alive in his heart and mind as well as being demonstrated in the real word. The sensory reality, the revelatory epiphany, and the written word all converged through the work of the Holy Spirit on that day. That's a paradigm I can live with.

TRANSFORMED BY HIS GLORY

The Apostle Paul learned that a man with a religious agenda can be changed instantly by the blinding presence of God. Gal. 1:9-12:

> "As we said before, so now I say again. If anyone preaches any other gospel to you than what you have received, let him be accursed. For do I now persuade men, or God? Or do I seek to please men? For if I still pleased men, I would not be a bondservant of Christ. But I make known to you, brethren, that the gospel which was preached by me is not according to man. For I neither received it from man, nor was I taught it, but it came through the revelation of Jesus Christ."

Paul, perhaps more than any other New Testament writer, understood the toxicity of a religious system built entirely on the traditions of men, the approval of men and the primacy of human wisdom. His was not a theoretical or intellectual argument. From first hand experience He recognized that true relationship with God flowed from the revelation of Jesus Christ. He knew well that the 'man-pleasing' spirit was anathema to the transformation that comes when the glory of God is manifest.

At the heart of religious dogma, there is always an ego driven agenda. The "man-pleasing spirit" is intertwined with a "self-pleasing" spirit; lust of the flesh, lust of the eyes, the pride of life. It starts off innocently enough with the need to be accepted, but quickly morphs into an overwhelming drive to get and keep people's approval. Ultimately, the 'fear of the Lord,' the sense that only His opinion counts, is lost. The focus shifts from a heavenly perspective to an earthly focus.

This spiritual perversion leads to all types of perversion in the natural. Religious leaders fall by the thousands to sexual immorality, financial misdeeds and raw power abuse. Ordinary believers find themselves trapped in systems and relationships that are not only nonproductive, but are actually destructive. The Church is decimated.

I remember vividly several years ago when a prominent pastor in Texas was exposed in serial homosexual activity. To his credit, he confessed openly his sins and submitted to counseling and restoration. What came out of his experience was very insightful. He said that he realized in counseling why he had been open to perversion and fallen so deeply in sin. The reason he gave for the fall in his life was the simple spiritual perversion that, to use his words, "I loved the Body more than the Head." His understanding of how the enemy gained entrance into his life was that he valued the Church, the people, more than Jesus. He sought their approval, he was working to please them. The good news is, he was set free. There is a way out!

When we truly see Jesus, He overshadows everything else—relationships, religion, sin, fear, failure—everything! It is only His approval we seek, and according to scripture, we already have that when we put our faith in Jesus Christ. When we walk with our focus on Jesus through the work of the Holy Spirit we are receiving a continuing flow of life-giving revelation coming directly from the Father. Our eyes are opened, not just to the folly of the human predicament, but to the transformational reality of His glory. The often quoted truth, *we become like what we behold*, becomes our reality. Jesus is formed in our inner man, and we are conformed in the outer.

GREATER WORKS

> "Verily, verily, I say unto you, He that believeth on me, the works that I do shall he do also; and greater works than these shall he do; because I go unto my Father." John 14:12 KJV

We have not been called to do the merely improbable, but the impossible. Jesus said that we would do the same works that He did. What were those works? The blind received their sight, lepers cleansed, deaf heard, lame walked, dead raised, demons cast out, storms stopped, water walked on, food multiplied and money taken from a fish's mouth. The same works would be difficult enough, but He said we would do greater works. Sounds like we need some help. To transition into the "greater" realm we have been given two keys. We are given the authority of Jesus' name, and we are given the Holy Spirit's power. In combination, these two factors release the Christian into the impossible (see John 14:13-19).

Most commentators on John 14:12 see the fulfillment of this word as being greater in number, not in kind. I'm not so sure the scripture makes that distinction. Jesus just said, "greater." Whatever greater means, Jesus said that the works that we would do would ultimately fulfill His mission and bring glory to the Father. This is true because whatever is done in His name is really done by Him.

Acts 10:38 tells us that; "...Jesus went about doing good, healing all who were oppressed of the devil..." While all charitable acts would be considered "good," what Jesus actually did was perform miraculous acts that could only be attributed to the anointing He had received from the Father. Jesus and the early Church advocated and practiced ministry to the widows, orphans and poor, but the real focus of what they did was release the power of the Holy Spirit to bring signs, wonders and miracles. As a matter of fact, I can't find one "good work" that Jesus did in the Gospels that didn't include a display of miraculous power.

Jesus said we'd do the same works, i.e., miracles, signs and wonders. These displays of supernatural power are the fulfillment of His promise, and He said that they would be "greater" than the works He did. Today an innumerable army of believers preach the unsearchable riches of Christ with demonstrations of power to confirm the Word. Untold numbers of people throughout the earth are seeing the miracle working power of Jesus delivering them from sin, sickness and the demonic on a daily basis. His Kingdom is coming and His will is being done on earth, TODAY! Recently, I have heard numerous testimonies from people who have had metal disappear from there bodies. The reports are from those who have had rods, pins, plates and screws surgically inserted for different medical reason. Several reports include the confirmation from doctors that the metal no longer shows up in X-rays or ultrasounds. Sounds pretty "great" to me!

THREE THINGS

Love & Power & Obedience

Jesus said His friends would be known by three defining characteristics; love, power and obedience.

> "A new commandment I give to you, that you love one another; as I have loved you, that you also love one another. By this all will know that you are My disciples, if you have love for one another." John 13:34-35

> "Most assuredly, I say to you, he who believes in Me, the works that I do he will do also; and greater works than these he will do, because I go to My Father. And whatever you ask in My name, that I will do, that the Father may be glorified in the Son. If you ask anything in My name I will do it." John 14:12-14

> "If you love Me, keep My commandments." John 14:15

> "He who has My commandments and keeps them, it is he who loves

> Me. And he who loves Me will be loved by My Father, and I will love him and manifest Myself to him."
> John 14:21

Love Never Fails

It is clear from reading the letters to the early Church that the primary contrast between the followers of Jesus and the world was to be their love for each other and honor for all men. God is love. The fruit of the Holy Spirit is love. When the Holy Spirit manifests Jesus to us, the first impression is love—His love for us and the atmosphere of love He releases in us. To walk in the Spirit is to walk in the love of God manifested. The love of God is imparted. It is genuine, not contrived. It flows from a secure relationship that allows the accepted to accept all others on the same basis.

You Shall Receive Power

Signs, wonders and miracles as well as the gifts of the Holy Spirit are never presented in scripture as optional accessories to the core message. They are integrated in the gospel and integral to its full presentation. Paul said that he had "fully preached" the gospel "through mighty signs and wonders, by the power of the Spirit of God" (Rom. 15:19). Jesus said, "...and these signs shall follow them that believe..." and the fulfillment came as they "went forth, and preached every where, the Lord working with them and confirming the word with signs following" (Mark 16:18-20).

The Power of Yes

Obedience to Jesus isn't legalism, it's saying yes to your lover. In our relationship based covenant we are motivated to "keep the words" of Jesus out of our desire to walk in the fulness of all that He has promised. We are not trying to earn approval, we are following a model that works—His. Grace is not permission to do whatever we want. Grace is the liberty to be and do all that He has released in us. Obedience to His Word fulfills our hearts' desire to be like Him.

TERRA FIRMA

> "For the earth is the Lord's, and the fulness thereof."
>
> 1 Corinthians 10:26

> "The earth is the LORD'S, and the fulness thereof, the world, and they that dwell therein. For He hath founded it upon the seas, and established it upon the floods."
> Psalm 24:1-2

> "Yes, I will rejoice over them to do them good, and I will assuredly plant them in this land, with all My heart and with all My soul."
>
> Jeremiah 32:41

God's connection to the land should be obvious to even the casual observer. He created it, established its boundaries and filled it with infinite variety and abundance. For His children, the children of promise, it is the designated place of blessing. It is our ground on which to stand. The very land itself is travailing in agreement with God's ultimate plan of revealing His children's full inheritance.

Our hope is not in a restoration of past blessings. Our present and future is the location of the fullness of all that has been promised. This is not a time to recapture memories of bygone days. This is the time to press into the fulfillment of all that has been prophesied over us. While much of the Kingdom of God is 'otherworldly,' the stage on which He has chosen to play out the eternal epic is *'terra firma.'*

David once cried out, "I would have fainted, unless I had believed to see the goodness of the LORD in the land of the living." Our God is the God of here and now: real time, real world blessing. His reach extends to the most remote unheralded regions. His strategy is to pour out His goodness, all of it, on you and your dwelling place. Can you grasp the concept that God has committed himself with

'ALL His heart and ALL His soul' found in Jeremiah 32:1? To what has He committed His all? He has committed to plant you in your land and to do you good. As a matter of fact, He rejoices in it. Now is the time to join in His festivities.

I believe God has prepared a place for every believer as 'fruitful ground.' This place is both spiritual and grounded in an earthly expression, a place for His goodness to be displayed. For the children of Israel the imperative was to arrive at that place at all cost. God's focus was on getting them to that place of fulfilled promise.

He has a place and a spiritual condition for you that is the earthly expression of the heavenly reality, the place of "Kingdom come" in your life. If you are dislocated from that place, now is the time to relocate. First your feet must be planted firmly on the solid rock of revelation. No storm can knock you off that rock. Out of the revelatory flow comes the stability of place, your place. He has one prepared for you.

In Christ, we are blessed with all the goodness of God. In Christ, we are the fulness of the earthly expression of the Kingdom. In Christ, we can do all things anywhere anytime. We are carrying the fulfillment of all of His promises wherever our feet touch the ground. Our task is to spread it around. Farmers employ two methods of planting seeds. One is where you put one seed in at a time in a specific place. The other is closer to the Kingdom methodology. Farmers call it "broadcasting." Seeds are scattered over ground and wherever they land is where they come up and bear fruit. God is broadcasting the seed of the Kingdom throughout the earth. Where it takes root and bears fruit is fruitful ground. Finding your fruitful ground is the destiny for which you have been prepared. Don't stop 'broadcasting' the seeds until you find the place that bears fruit.

HE CALLS YOU SON

Jesus was not a servant who aspired to be a son, He is the Son who chose to serve.

> "For you are all sons of God through faith in Christ Jesus...And because you are sons, God has sent forth the Spirit of His son into your hearts, crying out, 'Abba, Father!' Therefore you are no longer a slave but a son, and if a son, then an heir of God through Christ."
>
> Galatians 3:26; 4:6-7

A common theme in western movies has been the hired hand who replaces the son in the eyes of the patriarch of the ranch. In most cases this story line involves a weak or renegade son and a conniving but loyal cowboy who garners the father's affection in order to inherit the ranch. Jesus was not a servant working His way up the ladder. In the incarnation, Jesus is fully God—preexistent, eternal, the one by whom and for whom all things were created. He is the King of Glory, which makes it all the more remarkable that He chose to be a servant. He was not in a position of weakness trying to earn the Father's favor. His Father's full favor was already His.

The implications for us are liberating. He has decreed that all who follow Jesus in faith are also sons (and daughters), children of the most high. We don't have to earn that position, we couldn't if we tried. Our hearts have been in-dwelt by the same Spirit that was in Christ. Therefore, His Spirit within us cries out in all accuracy and honesty, *ABBA, Father*. The spirit of man draws back in unworthy self-loathing. The Spirit of God in us says, *YES, you are a son!* The change was brought about by God's initiative, not our own. God doesn't change His standards to accommodate man; He changes man to be an accommodation of His Spirit. We are transformed by His glory, conformed to His image and seated with Him in the heavenlies at the right hand of the Father. Resisting our inheritance is not simply an act of false humility, it is unbelief. On the cross Jesus paid the price and settled the issue. "For you are all sons of God through faith in Christ Jesus."

FULLY PREACHED

"Therefore in Christ Jesus I have
found reason for boasting in things

> pertaining to God. For I will not presume to speak of anything except what Christ has accomplished through me, resulting in the obedience of the Gentiles by word and deed, in the power of signs and wonders, in the power of the Spirit; so that from Jerusalem and round about as far as Illyricum I have fully preached the gospel of Christ."
> Romans 15:17-19

Today an almost universal movement in the western Church exists to eliminate the offensive elements from the presentation of the gospel. The concept is to make the church experience non-threatening and as pleasant for unbelievers as possible. On the surface it sounds good. The problem is that in seeking to become user friendly (seeker sensitive) we are becoming Holy Spirit hostile. Sunday morning worship services have become multimedia presentations timed to the minute with no room for the Holy Spirit to work. Gifts and manifestations of the Spirit are forbidden. The use of drama and other arts, as well as all types of media are a wonderful way to get the message across. So is preaching. However, without the opportunity for people to experience the transformational power of the Holy Spirit they have not truly encountered the gospel. The Apostle Paul considered the gospel "fully preached" because the message was presented with mighty signs and wonders. Mark 16:20 says that the early believers "went forth everywhere, the Lord working with them, and confirming the word with signs following."

In many churches that profess a belief in the supernatural there is no place in meetings for the miraculous to be demonstrated. The real danger in this form of presentation is that there is no encounter with the power of God. The scripture is clear that without the work of the Holy Spirit there is no "new birth." Are we simply repeating the sins of our fathers who filled buildings with unregenerate people?

What most American churches want is a "spokesmodel," not the biblical design. The early apostles, prophets, evangelists, even Jesus himself, would not be welcome in most modern fellowships. Their emphasis on miracles, signs and wonders would be considered excessive. Paul was clear in his first letter to the Corinthians that the practice of the gifts of the Spirit is the core of what the Body of Christ is all about. I would go so far as to say that in the early Church the gifts of the Spirit were the structure. The Church was not organized by a flow chart or by constitutional charter, instead it was structured by the gifts of the Spirit working through individuals for the mutual edification of all. The heart of every meeting was the presence of God manifested by the work of the Holy Spirit. The order of service was the exercising of the gifts through every believer. By eliminating the personal working of the Holy Spirit from our meetings we have devolved into what Paul described in 2 Timothy 3:5 as "having a form of godliness, but denying the power thereof."

While conducting meetings in Fiji, I instructed the people to talk to their hands. I led them through an exercise of speaking to their hands and saying, "Hand, I'm gonna lay you on some sick people and they are going to get well." Everyone laughed and enjoyed the point. The pastor's two-and-a-half year old granddaughter was in the meeting. The following night her brother was sitting in his grandmothers lap sick with fever. The little girl wanted him to come and play, but he was really too sick to be in the service much less get up and play. She walked up to her brother and said "Hand, I'm gonna lay you on the sick." She then laid her hand on him and said, "In Jesus name, sickness, go!" Guess what? He got up healed, with no fever and began to play with his sister and the other kids. Even the least among us can demonstrate the love and power of Jesus Christ when we allow the anointing of the Holy Spirit the opportunity to work.

> "For am I now seeking the favor of men, or of God? Or am I striving to please men? If I were still trying to please men, I would not be a bond-servant of Christ."
>
> Galatians 1:10

GLOBAL WEIRDING AND WOLVES

I watched with interest news reports about dead birds falling from the sky, unusually large fish kills, extreme weather events like flooding in Australia and severe blizzards in the U.S. and Europe. The term "global warming" doesn't seem to fit, so I refer to these extreme events as "global weirding." My local community has experienced a manifestation of global weirding in our coyote population.

Encountering coyotes in Texas is not unusual, even in urban areas where we live. However, what is unusual is that these coyotes have become very aggressive. The police have been called recently when the pack chased a pizza delivery guy back to his car trying to take the pizza right out of his hands. A day or so later, this same group of coyotes attacked a poodle being walked by its owner near her townhouse. What they didn't achieve with the pizza, they apparently did with the poodle—dinner.

With the coyotes in mind I read this scripture this morning from Acts 20:29: "For I know this, that after my departure savage wolves will come in among you, not sparing the flock." Paul was warning the Ephesian Church that those would be coming who would subvert the "gospel of grace" that he preached. He compared them to wolves who would savagely try to separate the people and devour them.

Who are the wolves?

The first mention of wolves in the Bible is found in Ezekiel 22:27. The prophet brings the word of the Lord against corrupt Jerusalem where the priests, prophets and princes are compared to wild beast tearing their prey, shedding their blood and destroying their souls, all for dishonest gain. The same charge is echoed in Zephaniah 3:3. In Matthew 7:15 Jesus identifies false prophets as those who come in sheep's clothing but are actually blood thirsty wolves. Jesus warned the twelve and the seventy as they were sent out that they were being sent as "sheep among wolves." The wolves are identified by their fruit according to Matt. 7:16. In short, wolves are false leaders who are out for their own gain at your expense.

What are they trying to do?

In agreement with the enemy, their prototype, they draw believers away, then disable them, destroying their soul in the process, all for dishonest gain. Satan comes to steal, kill, and destroy, so their pattern is the same. They seek to build their own kingdoms by tearing down the Kingdom.

How do you deal with wolves?

Scripture says we are to beware, alert and mindful of these false "leaders." Our posture is to be as "wise as serpents and harmless as doves." Warned and aware of the danger, we are to "go," according to Luke 10:3, and carry out our biblical mandate to preach and demonstrate the Kingdom. We must not "shrink back" or be intimidated by their tactics (2 Tim 1:7). Since the wolves in Paul's warning are specifically identified as those who would put the people of God back under the law, his word in Galatians 3 would apply; "Who has bewitched you?" Apparently the Galatian believers had already fallen victim to their tactics. We are not to be distracted or diverted by their words. They will seek to move you from grace back under a system of works and law—man's efforts, accomplishments, plans and procedures—to achieve their true motive, which is to enslave you for their own ego and monetary gain.

The focus of the biblical admonitions is this—you are free so stay free. Carry out the mission the Church has been assigned. Go into all the earth and preach the gospel of the Kingdom with signs, wonders and miracles confirming the Word. Don't be shut down, distracted, diverted or discouraged by those who seek to manipulate the people of God for their own purposes. It was for freedom you were set free, let no man put the yokes of bondage on your shoulders ever again!

Chapter 7

Portals of Glory

> *portal* (noun) 1. a doorway, gate or other entrance. 2. COMPUTING: an internet site providing access or links to other sites.

In science fiction the concept of a specific place or object being used to provide access to another dimension is a quite common literary device. For example, in C.S. Lewis' *Chronicles of Narnia* a wardrobe is the entrance into the fantasy world of Narnia. On the spiritual side, many religions regard holy places as locations where the veil between the material world and the supernatural world is "very thin." In the world of computing, a portal is an internet site used to gain access to other sites or it is the place where you plug in the connections on the computer itself.

Recently I had the privilege of ministering at a new church on the Sunshine Coast of Australia that is alive with people who are passionately pressing in to see a move of God to change their region and their nation. In the supercharged atmosphere of aggressive hunger, I heard the Spirit of the Lord say to the people, "YOU are a portal of my glory."

The more I meditate on that word, the more I realize it is a universal truth for the Body of Christ in this season. We are called to be the point of connection and access to the glory realm. The prophet Haggai refers to a point in human history when God would raise up a temple for the purpose of filling it with His glory. This "latter house glory" is described as being greater glory. When coupled with Peter's words about being the habitation of God and Paul's declaration that we are the temple of the Holy Spirit, it is clear that we are walking, breathing, talking vessels of the glory of God. When others encounter Jesus in us, they are "beholding the glory of the Father."

We are in an interactive mode with the glory realm through the work of the Holy Spirit. Jesus is our access, the door—the portal for us. As we enter into that realm we are transformed into glory outlets for the display of His glory in all the earth. The thought is really staggering. We not only behold His glory, in the words of Paul, we become what we behold. The completion of that transformation comes as we begin to shine for others with the same glory we have received. YOU are a glory portal.

For all of our passion for Jesus, the power of the Holy Spirit and the manifested glory of the Father, we will do more harm than good if we carry only the teaching and not the reality. As believers we have continual uninterrupted access into the throne room of the Father. Beholding the face of Jesus through the revelatory work of the Holy Spirit, we become what we behold.

AN ISLAND EXPERIENCE

> "And the Word became flesh and dwelt among us, and we beheld His glory, the glory as of the only begotten of the Father, full of grace and truth."
>
> John 1:1

Several years ago I had the unique experience of going to the Solomon Islands to minister with a group that is truly a "revival tribe." Over the years, the *Are' Are'* of the remote southern area of Malaita, have experienced repeated waves of revival with many unusual signs and wonders always a major part of the moves. They have seen the dead raised, countless healing miracles, and something I experienced myself on one occasion; a non-English speaking prophet breaking into perfect Oxford diction to deliver a 100% accurate word with details impossible to know apart from the unction of the Holy Spirit.

Over 700 people had traveled for days to be in this particular meeting either on foot or in the cargo hold of an ancient freighter. The long narrow meeting house had no electricity and no chairs, only benches made of teak planks sitting on rocks or blocks. The inside of the building was packed and the open sides revealed several hundred people who couldn't get in despite the crowd being packed shoulder to shoulder.

As I was preaching I heard the Spirit of the Lord say, "Be quiet, wait on Me." So I gave the instruction to the people to wait on the Lord in silence. A holy hush instantly fell on the crowd. No babies cried, no dogs barked and no rooster crowed in the village. It was a supernatural silence. This went on for quite some time and I had no idea what God was about to do, but I waited. As I walked up and down the long center aisle of the wooden tabernacle, the only thing I saw happening was a single tear drop trickling down the face of one young woman. The moment I saw the tear on the young woman's face, something happened. She let out a scream at the top of her lungs that was like nothing I had ever heard. In the silence of the moment the effect was startling and instantaneous. As soon as she let out the scream the whole place erupted in what I can only describe now as a Holy Ghost riot. The people began to shout, they began to run and, yes, even began to jump over the "pews." One man began to roll across the floor at the front of the building from one side to another with impossible speed and seemingly no effort on his part whatsoever. Several old ladies in the group began to run up and down the center aisle like Olympic sprinters. Spontaneous praise broke out that no worship leader could ever hope to orchestrate. It was literally pandemonium.

All I could do was stand with my back up against a wall at the front and watch as this incredible event unfolded.

The fire and fervor showed no signs of abating, but I was curious; what had happened to the young woman with the tear and the scream that had set this off? I dispatched my translator to go and ask her what had happened to her that triggered this radical outburst. I sent him for two reasons, one was because he spoke the language, but also because I was afraid to try to cross the aisle and get run over by the sprinting grannies. After a long time he came back to me to report what she said, "She said she saw Jesus." I thought that was a good explanation but he continued, "She said she didn't see Jesus as a baby in a manger or Jesus on the cross. She said she saw Jesus like John saw Jesus on the Isle of Patmos (*Revelation 1:10ff*)." It hit me like a ton of bricks. She didn't see Jesus in the past, she saw Jesus as He is now; glorified, seated on the throne, full of power and majesty, the reigning King of Glory. The immediate effect of this one young woman seeing Jesus revealed in His glory was to set off a Holy Spirit outpouring like none other I have ever witnessed. Jesus got real to her that night!

WHAT ARE YOU EXPECTING?

A significant element to the outpouring of the Holy Spirit on the Day of Pentecost, and the subsequent signs, wonders and miracles, was the fact that they gathered intentionally for that express purpose. They were following the instructions of Jesus, seeking the outpouring of the Holy Spirit, even though at that point they had no previous experience of that type of event—no one had! They gathered "in one accord," on purpose, with an expectation of the promise being fulfilled in their lives

What are you expecting today? What are you asking for? Are you seeking the reality of His glory in your life? Unfortunately, many people lower their expectations to fit their current earthbound reality. It is critical that we see beyond our situations and ourselves, beyond our limits to the unlimited promises, power and provision of God. That comes by revelation. As it is written: "Eye has not seen, nor ear heard, Nor have entered into the heart of man The things which God has prepared for those who love Him. ***But God has revealed them to us through His Spirit*** (1 Cor. 2:9-10)."

The Spirit of God flowing from His throne is referred to in Ezekiel 47 and Revelation 22 as a river. The description in Ezekiel states that the farther he went in the river, the deeper and wider it got. Jesus refers to the river springing up in us as a continual flow. Both examples indicate a never-ending and ever-increasing flow. Paul referred to our experience with the glory of God as being "from glory to glory." Whatever you have already experienced of the glory of the Father, there is still more. More realms, more depth, more of Jesus. I want more. The prayer I have repeated, too many times to count in hundreds of places all over the world, is still my prayer today; "Lord, we are your temple. Lord, I am your temple. Fill your temple with your glory—NOW."

Made in the USA
Charleston, SC
04 April 2013